Education at a Crossroads

What Works and What's Wasted in Education Today

Subcommittee Report

Subcommittee on Oversight and Investigations
of the
Committee on Education and the Workforce
U.S. House of Representatives
One Hundred Fifth Congress
Second Session
July 17, 1998

WILLIAM F. GOODLING, Pennsylvania, *Chairman*

THOMAS E. PETRI, Wisconsin
MARGE ROUKEMA, New Jersey
HARRIS W. FAWELL, Illinois
CASS BALLENGER, North Carolina
BILL E. BARRETT, Nebraska
PETER HOEKSTRA, Michigan
HOWARD P. "BUCK" McKEON, California
MICHAEL N. CASTLE, Delaware
SAM JOHNSON, Texas
JAMES M. TALENT, Missouri
JAMES C. GREENWOOD, Pennsylvania
JOSEPH K. KNOLLENBERG, Michigan
FRANK D. RIGGS, California
LINDSEY O. GRAHAM, South Carolina
MARK E. SOUDER, Indiana
DAVID M. McINTOSH, Indiana
CHARLIE W. NORWOOD, JR., Georgia
RON PAUL, Texas
BOB SCHAFFER, Colorado
JOHN E. PETERSON, Pennsylvania
FRED UPTON, Michigan
NATHAN DEAL, Georgia
VAN HILLEARY, Tennessee
MIKE PARKER, Mississippi

WILLIAM (BILL) CLAY, Missouri
GEORGE MILLER, California
DALE E. KILDEE, Michigan
MATTHEW G. MARTINEZ, California
MAJOR R. OWENS, New York
DONALD M. PAYNE, New Jersey
PATSY MINK, Hawaii
ROBERT E. ANDREWS, New Jersey
TIM ROEMER, Indiana
ROBERT C. "BOBBY" SCOTT, Virginia
LYNN C. WOOLSEY, California
CARLOS A. ROMERO-BARCELO, Puerto-Rico
CHAKA FATTAH, Pennsylvania
RUBEN HINOJOSA, Texas
CAROLYN McCARTHY, New York
JOHN F. TIERNEY, Massachusetts
RON KIND, Wisconsin
LORETTA SANCHEZ, California
HAROLD E. FORD, JR., Tennessee
DENNIS KUCINICH, Ohio

Kevin Talley, *Staff Director*
Gail E. Weiss, *Minority Staff Director*

SUBCOMMITTEE ON OVERSIGHT AND INVESTIGATIONS

PETER HOEKSTRA, Michigan, *Chairman*

CHARLIE W. NORWOOD, JR., Georgia
VAN HILLEARY, Tennessee
CASS BALLENGER, North Carolina
BOB SCHAFFER, Colorado
MIKE PARKER, Mississippi

PATSY MINK, Hawaii
ROBERT C. SCOTT, Virginia
RON KIND, Wisconsin
HAROLD E. FORD, JR., Tennessee

Preamble

The Subcommittee on Oversight and Investigations of the Committee on Education and the Workforce considered this report on July 17, 1998. A quorum being present, the report was favorably adopted by a vote of 5 to 2.

TABLE OF CONTENTS

PREAMBLE III

ACKNOWLEDGMENTS IX

INTRODUCTION XI

EXECUTIVE SUMMARY XI

AT THE CROSSROADS OF EXCELLENCE, MEDIOCRITY AND FAILURE 1
    BIRTH OF THE "CROSSROADS PROJECT" 8
    GAO REPORT ON BEST PRACTICES 9
    FINDING SUCCESS IN CHICAGO 9

THE FEDERAL ROLE IN EDUCATION: BUREAUCRACY VS. CHILDREN 10
    JUST HOW LARGE IS THE FEDERAL EDUCATION BUREAUCRACY? 10
    760 FEDERAL EDUCATION PROGRAMS…AND COUNTING 11
    IT TAKES A VILLAGE TO COMPLETE THE PAPERWORK 15
        Ohio: 50 percent of Paperwork for Six Percent of Funds 15
        25,000 Paperwork Employees 15
        A Nine-Pound Application "Birthed" in Boston 15
        65 Cents on the Dollar? 17
        Enough is Enough 19
    THE 487-STEP LABYRINTH: GOVERNMENT ATTEMPTS TO REINVENT ITSELF 20
    COSTLY REQUIREMENTS AND REGULATIONS 20
    SCORES OF PROGRAMS FOR EVERY PROBLEM 20
    BAYWATCH AND JERRY SPRINGER: YOUR TAX DOLLARS AT WORK 22
    ON THE PLAYGROUND WITH THE FEDERAL GOVERNMENT 22
    OTHER "EDUCATIONAL" PUBLICATIONS FROM THE DEPARTMENT OF EDUCATION 23
    FEDERALLY FUNDED "HOLIDAY AWARENESS" 23
    FRAUGHT WITH FAILURE 25
    A COMPLETE LACK OF EVIDENCE OF EFFECTIVENESS 25
    LACK OF FOLLOW-THROUGH 26
    INEFFECTIVE ASSISTANCE 27

THE CROSSROADS PROJECT: FINDING SUCCESS AT THE LOCAL LEVEL 30
    PARENTS INVOLVED IN THEIR CHILDREN'S EDUCATION 32
    LOCAL CONTROL, LOCAL ACCOUNTABILITY 43
    MASTERING THE BASICS 47
    DOLLARS FOR CLASSROOMS, NOT BUREAUCRATS 52

BEYOND CROSSROADS: WHAT WE LEARNED, THE ROAD AHEAD 56
    THE FEDERAL ROLE: SUPPORTING WHAT WORKS 56
        EMPOWER PARENTS 57
        RETURN CONTROL TO THE LOCAL LEVEL 59
        ENCOURAGE BASIC ACADEMICS 60
        SEND DOLLARS TO THE CLASSROOM 60
    REFORMING THE FEDERAL ROLE FOR THE 21ST CENTURY 61

Table of Contents, continued

Appendix A... A1
Appendix B... B1
Appendix C... C1
Appendix D... D1
Appendix E... E1

Minority Views.. 1

List of Figures

Figure 1	Trends in NAEP Reading Scores for the Nation
Figure 2	On Budget Federal Funds for Elementary and Secondary Education vs. NAEP Reading Scores
Figure 3	Half of All Urban High School Students fail to graduate in four Years, If At All
Figure 4	Percent of Students Scoring At or Above "Basic" Level on NAEP
Figure 5	Percent of 8th graders Who Attend Schools Where School Officials Say Lack of Parent Involvement is a Moderate or Serious Problem
Figure 6	Older Students Have Fallen Behind International Averages in Math and Science
Figure 7	Bureaucracy vs. Children: America's Choice in Education
Figure 8	Number of State Employees Needed to Administer $1 Billion in Government Spending
Figure 9	Three Target Groups Served by Multiple Programs and Agencies
Figure 10	Location of Crossroads Field Hearings

List of Tables

Table 1	12th Grade: U.S. Lags Behind in Math and Science
Table 2	Federal Education Spending: 1997
Table 3	For Every Dollar Sent to Washington for Department of Education Elementary and Secondary Education Programs, Only $.85 Is Received by Local Education Agencies
Table 4	Percent of States and School Districts who Reported Fed Supported Technical Assistance Centers and Labs to be Either "Not at All Helpful" or Only "A Little Helpful"
Table 5	Percentage of Parents of Students in Grades 3-12 Who Were Satisfied With Aspects of Their Child's School: 1993
Table 6	South Carolina Tracks Dollars to the Classroom

List of Appendices

Appendix A	Education at a Crossroads: Hearing Witnesses
Appendix B	Superintendent Survey
Appendix C	Federal Education Spending: 1965-1997
Appendix D	Cost of Crossroads Hearings
Appendix E	788 Education Programs - Statistics & Breakdown

Acknowledgments

The Chairman wishes to thank the hundreds of people who made this project possible:

- Parents and students who gave thoughtful testimony concerning their experiences with what works and what is wasted in education.

- Teachers who provided a front line view of what works in the classroom.

- Principals, administrators and staff of schools around the country, who graciously opened their doors to host Subcommittee hearings and demonstrate what is working in education today.

- State education officials whose input presented the Subcommittee with valuable insight into the administration of federal education programs.

- Policy experts and federal officials who brought familiarity and in-depth knowledge with education programs to the hearings.

- The staff of the House of Representatives Committee on Education and the Workforce who put in untold hours of work on this project, and without whom, the Crossroads project could not have succeeded.

- The many community leaders and activists, business owners and everyday citizens who have attended hearings and made their experiences available to the Subcommittee.

In giving their time and testimony, the individuals mentioned above have each contributed to an important debate in our country: how to improve education. Creating and maintaining the best education system in the world will require nothing less than the commitment of more individuals like those who have been involved in this project. These individuals all deserve credit for their contributions.

INTRODUCTION

The Subcommittee on Oversight and Investigations, in accordance with Rule X of the U.S. House of Representatives,[1] undertook an intensive review of the federal role in education. This review, which included extensive visits to schools across the country, is the only known such review ever performed by the Committee or by Congress.

EXECUTIVE SUMMARY

America's educational system is at a crossroads. Down one path can be found the many successful schools and systems that have emerged from the crisis of the 1980s to become shining examples of educational excellence. Down the other path are schools that are mired in failure or that have implemented erroneous reforms, succeeding only in worsening their already dismal performances. At the intersection of these two paths are the vast majority of America's schools – stagnating in mediocrity – at the crossroads of excellence and failure.

The purpose of the Committee on Education and the Workforce's Crossroads project was to identify the steps that lead in the direction of either excellence or failure in order to develop a positive vision for change. At a time when the economy continues to grow and technological advancements of the information age are fundamentally changing how we live and work, our nation should not be willing to accept mediocrity in education. America needs to develop a world class education system that is second to none. In order to succeed, our education system must have flexibility and vision - a willingness to think and act "outside of the box"- for the sake of our children.

Since the seminal report *A Nation at Risk* was released in 1983 describing the "rising tide of mediocrity" in America's schools, there have been some improvements. More students than ever are going on to college. SAT scores have risen moderately and fourth grade students have performed well on international comparison tests. However, despite these few bright spots, current indicators paint a disappointing picture overall of the preparedness of today's students to continue our nation's economic strength well into the 21st century.

- 40 percent of fourth-graders do not read at even a basic level;[2]
- Half of the students from urban school districts fail to graduate on time, if at all;[3]
- Average 1996 NAEP scores among 17-year-olds are lower than they were in

---

[1] Robin H. Carle, Clerk of the House of Representatives, *Rules of the House of Representatives, Effective for One Hundred Fifth Congress*, January 7, 1997.
[2] National Center for Education Statistics, *NAEP 1994 Reading Report Card for the Nation and the States*, U.S. Department of Education, March 1996.
[3] *Ibid.*

1984, a year after *A Nation at Risk* was released;
- U.S. 12th graders only outperformed two out of 21 nations in mathematics;[4]
- American students fall farther behind students from other countries the longer they are in school;[5]
- Public institutions of higher education annually spend $1 billion on remedial education.[6]

The factors behind stagnant scores and declining international performance must be addressed to ensure that U.S. students are competitive in a global marketplace when they graduate.

For more than 40 years, the federal government has been increasingly influential in local schooling. Since 1957, when the Soviet Union launched the Sputnik satellite, federal education spending and red tape has been expanding and becoming more involved in the classroom. Since 1980, nearly $400 billion has been spent by the federal government on education.

A key decision at the crossroads: It is time for America to take a careful look at what billions of federal education dollars have purchased, and to make hard decisions about whether to continue expanding the federal role, or to return control to parents and teachers.

The Crossroads project began in 1995 as a project of the House Education and Workforce Committee's Subcommittee on Oversight and Investigations, under the leadership of Chairman Pete Hoekstra. Its mission was to answer the following questions about education:

1. What are the elements of a successful school?
2. To what extent do federal education programs contribute or detract from those factors?
3. What works and what is wasted?

After asking the General Accounting Office (GAO) to determine the elements of successful schools, the Subcommittee began a series of hearings around the country to look at what works and what is wasted at the local level.[7] The Subcommittee traveled to 15 states and heard from more than 225 witnesses. These hearings gave principals,

---

[4] *Ibid.*
[5] *Ibid.*
[6] David W. Breneman, "The Extent and Cost of Remediation in Higher Education," *Brookings Papers on Education Policy,* Washington, D.C.: The Brookings Institution, April, 1998.
[7] U.S. General Accounting Office, *Schools and Workplaces: An Overview of Successful and Unsuccessful Practices,* GAO/PEMD-95-28, August, 1995, p. 3.

teachers, parents, students and state officials from around the country a rare opportunity to share their experiences about what works and what is wasted. Rather than relying on a small, elite group of witnesses who could leave their work to come to Washington and testify, the Subcommittee visited educators, parents and students where learning takes place: the classroom. From small towns to major cities, real people discussed real successes and problems in education. Apart from these hearings, these voices may never have been heard.

Based on the findings of GAO and these hearings, the Subcommittee found that successful schools and school systems were not the product of federal funding and programs, but instead were characterized by:

- Parents involved in the education of their children;
- Local control;
- Emphasis on basic academics;
- Dollars spent on the classroom, not bureaucracy and ineffective programs.

The Current Federal Role

In addition to these findings, the Crossroads project researched the nature of the current federal role in education. The Committee found a system fraught with failure and bureaucracy:

- **More than 760 federal education programs:** For the first time in the history of federal education funding, the Committee assembled the most comprehensive list of federal education programs to date. At least 39 federal agencies oversee more than 760 education programs, at a cost of $100 billion a year to taxpayers. The Congressional Research Service has confirmed that these numbers are accurate, and even added additional programs to the 760 originally found by the committee.

    The leviathan of federal education programs has actually led to a cottage industry in selling information on program descriptions, application deadlines and filing instructions for each of the myriad of federal education programs. The Education Funding Research Council identifies potential sources of funds for local school districts, and sells for nearly $400 the *Guide to Federal Funding for Education*. The company promises to steer its subscribers to "a wide range of Federal programs," and offers these subscribers timely updates on "500 education programs." More recently, the *Aid for Education Report* published by CD Publications advertised that "huge sums are available…in the federal government alone, there are nearly 800 different education programs that receive authorization totaling almost a hundred billion dollars."

- **Mountains of Paperwork:** Even after accounting for recent reductions, the U.S. Department of Education still requires over 48.6 million hours worth of paperwork per year - or the equivalent of 25,000 employees working full-time.[8] The Subcommittee has attempted to quantify the number of pages required by recipients of federal funds in order to qualify for assistance. Without fully accounting for all the attachments and supplemental submissions required with each application, the Committee counted more than 20,000 pages of applications states must fill out to receive federal education funds each year.

- **A "Shadow" Department of Education:** The Department of Education touts that it is one of the smallest federal agencies with 4,637 employees, and that it has a relatively small administrative budget. What many people do not realize, however, is that there are nearly three times as many federally funded employees of state education agencies administering federal education programs, as there are U.S. Department of Education employees. According to GAO, there are about 13,400 FTEs (full-time equivalents) funded with federal dollars to administer these programs for state education agencies.

- **As little as 65-70 cents reaches the classroom:** A recent study found that for every tax dollar sent to Washington for elementary and secondary education, 85 cents is returned to local school districts. The remaining 15 cents is spent on bureaucracy and national and research programs of unknown effectiveness.[9] The Department of Education has since released a study, which also found that about 85 cents of federal dollars reaches school districts for use in the classroom.[10] Although these studies provided information not previously available on federal education spending, they only examined what was returned to school districts, still several layers of bureaucracy away from the classroom.

  To date, no studies exist to enable us to determine what portion of federal education dollars actually reach the classroom, or what schools and state education agencies must spend to apply for education dollars and comply with their requirements. However, audits of school district spending indicate just how little in general reaches the classroom. A recent audit of the New York City School District found that only 43 percent of the district's total funds were spent on direct classroom expenditures.[11]

---

[8] Marshall Smith, "Paper Reduction Act Accomplishments and Plans for Future," U.S. Department of Education, October 31, 1996.

[9] Christine L. Olson, *U.S. Department of Education Financing of Elementary and Secondary Education: Where the Money Goes*, (Washington, DC: The Heritage Foundation), December 30, 1996.

[10] U.S. Department of Education, Planning and Evaluation Service, *The Use of Federal Education Funds for Administrative Costs*, 1998, p. 28.

[11] Jacques Steinberg, "NYC School System Budget Analysis Shows 43% Goes to Classroom," *The New York Times*, November 21, 1996. See also: Speakman, Cooper, Sampiere, May, Holsomback, Glass, "Bringing Money to the Classroom: A Systemic Resource Model Applied to the New York City Public

Given the 48.6 million paperwork hours required to receive federal education dollars and the school district bureaucracies funds must pass through to reach the classroom, it is not unreasonable to assume that another 15- 20 cents spent outside the classroom. This would mean a net return of 65-70 cents to the classroom.

- **The 487 Step Labyrinth:** In 1993, Vice-President Gore's National Performance Review discovered that the Department of Education's discretionary grant process lasted 26 weeks and took 487 steps from start to finish. It was not until 1996 that the Department finally took steps to begin "streamlining" their long and protracted grant review process, a process that has yet to be completed and fully implemented. After the streamlining is complete it will *only* take an average of 20 weeks and 216 steps to complete a review.[12]

- **Federal Dollars for *Baywatch* and *Jerry Springer*:** The Department of Education's Office of Special Education and Rehabilitative Services Media and Captioning Services funds closed captioning for "educational" programs such as *Baywatch, Ricki Lake, The Montel Williams Show,* and *Jerry Springer.* By funding captioning for these programs - funding which could easily be provided by the television industry or other commercial enterprises - the federal government is demonstrating to the American people just how far away it is from supporting what works and identifying federal education priorities.

Programs for Every Problem

The massive array of federal education programs was not created overnight, but developed slowly, as an attempt to address specific problems. Each program received minimal funding at the outset, and most have received additional funds from one year to the next. The current arrangement of federal education funding is as follows: local tax dollars go to Washington, where they are allocated to a variety of purposes, usually to address what someone in the federal government sees as a problem. The money is then returned to states and school districts in the form of categorical programs. This process puts smaller school districts at a disadvantage: States and local school districts are highly dependent on administrators and skilled grant writers to obtain these federal dollars and comply with their requirements, which places a greater burden on poorer and smaller school systems.

The effectiveness of these programs is seldom measured, even as the problems continue to mount. Evaluations of federal programs almost always measure process, not

---

Schools," *Where Does the Money Go? Resource Allocation in Elementary and Secondary Schools*, Lawrence O. Picus and James L. Wattenberger, eds., (Thosand Oaks, CA: Corwin Press, 1995).
[12] U.S. Department of Education Report, "A Redesigned Discretionary Grant Process" - Vice President Gore's National Performance Review 1995. Redesigned process is due to be in place in 1998.

whether or not they help children learn. For example, the largest education program for disadvantaged children has spent more than $100 billion over 30 years while producing hardly any evidence of positive, lasting results. Congress must ensure that such wasteful use of tax dollars is stopped.

It is time for the burden of proof to shift to the federal government. **If it cannot be demonstrated that a particular federal program is more effectively spending funds than state and local communities would otherwise spend them, Congress should return the money to the states and the people, without any burdensome strings attached.** This Subcommittee has found little evidence proving the effectiveness of federal programs, or that federal programs are more effective than local efforts.

Now is the time to act on what we've learned. The central theme of what we learned is that the federal government cannot consistently and effectively replicate success stories throughout the nation in the form of federal programs. Instead, federal education dollars should support effective state and local initiatives, ensuring that it neither impedes local innovation and control, nor diverts dollars from the classroom through burdensome regulations and overhead.

Empower Parents
- Reduce the family federal tax burden;
- Encourage parental choice in education at all levels of government;
- Create opportunity scholarships for poor children in Washington, D.C., and other federal empowerment zones;
- Allow states to send Title I (Aid to Disadvantaged Students) funds to impoverished parents as grants in order to enable their children to receive additional academic assistance.

Return Control to the Local Level
- Return federal elementary and secondary education funds to states and local school districts through flexible grants;
- Expand opportunities for waivers from burdensome regulations;
- Give states and school districts greater freedom to consolidate program funds to more effectively address pressing needs;
- Provide no-strings-attached funds for charter school start-up costs.

Encourage What Works in the Classroom
- Federally funded education programs should only use proven methods backed by reliable, replicable research;
- Research and evaluation should concentrate on measuring outcomes and less on process—such as how many children are served by a particular program.

Send Dollars to the Classroom
- Streamline and consolidate federal education programs;
- Reform or eliminate ineffective and inefficient programs;
- Reduce paperwork burden.

Fifteen years ago our nation was diagnosed as being at risk - at risk of entering the 21st Century lagging behind other industrialized nations economically and educationally. Since then there has been little evidence of the federal government effectively addressing this problem through its hundreds of duplicative and uncoordinated education programs.

In order to address the continued crisis, education policy in this country needs to be re-oriented around ensuring that children receive a quality education, not preserving programs and bureaucracies. Significant progress needs to be made by all levels of government: Solving problems at the federal level is only one component.

Congress has already begun to take action. The findings of the Crossroads Project have underscored an education agenda that has encouraged "flex" grants, parental choice in education, education savings accounts, scholarships for low income children, charter schools, and getting dollars to the classroom.

The federal government should only play a limited role in education: It should serve education at the state and local level as a research and statistics gathering agency, disseminating findings and enabling states to share best practices with each other. Local educators must be empowered to teach children with effective methods and adequate resources, without federal interference. Parents must once again be in charge of the education of their children. Schools should be havens for learning, safe from drugs and violence.

Much work remains. It is time for the federal bureaucracy to move out of the way- to put children first - by supporting what works. The Crossroads Report points the way.

AT THE CROSSROADS OF EXCELLENCE, MEDIOCRITY AND FAILURE

In 1983, then Secretary of Education Terrel Bell and the National Commission on Excellence in Education released the report, *A Nation at Risk*.[1] In this report, the commission described the "rising tide of mediocrity" in American education and warned of the dire consequences that would surely result if the educational establishment didn't quickly change course. This, in many ways, marked the beginning of an educational reform movement that has achieved many noteworthy successes but, unfortunately, has yet to produce a system that provides an excellent and truly equitable education for all children. Many of the recommendations of the report went unheeded, which recently led education leaders and former members of the Commission to conclude that "vast institutions don't change because they should…[t]hey change only when they must."[2]

Today, America's educational system is at a crossroads. Down one path can be found the many successful schools and systems that have emerged from the "rising tide of mediocrity" of the early 1980s to become shining examples of educational excellence. Down the other path are schools that are mired in failure or that have implemented erroneous reforms, succeeding only in worsening their already dismal performances. At the intersection of these two paths are the vast majority of America's schools – stagnating in mediocrity – at the crossroads of excellence and failure.

Recent statistics paint a stark picture of the continued crisis in American education:

A semi-literate nation:

- Forty percent of fourth-graders do not read at even a basic level.[3] Fifty-seven percent of urban students score below the basic level.

- A 1992 survey by the Department of Education found that between 21 to 23 percent, or about 40 million of the 191 million adults in this country, are in the bottom of five literacy assessment proficiency categories. This means that nearly one in four adults has such rudimentary reading and writing skills that they would not be able to write a letter to their credit card company about a mistake in their bill.

---

[1] *A Nation At Risk* outlined risk indicators such as: 13 percent of all 17-year-olds were functionally illiterate (today 25 percent score below basic on NAEP proficiency tests). The Commission proposed reforming the education system in fundamental ways in the areas of content, teaching, standards, the use of time, leadership, and fiscal support.

[2] *A Nation Still at Risk: An Education Manifesto*, April 30, 1998. This manifesto resulted from a meeting of prominent education reformers, business leaders and policy makers sponsored by The Center for Education Reform, Empower America, The Heritage Foundation and The Thomas B. Fordham Foundation.

[3] National Center for Education Statistics, *NAEP 1994 Reading Report Card for the Nation and the States*, U.S. Department of Education, March 1996.

- Almost 50 percent of the nation's adults performed at the bottom two of the five categories.[4] Sixty-eight percent of the nation's adult prison population read and write at the bottom two out of five proficiency levels.[5]

Failing Education Systems in Urban America

- Forty-nine percent of teachers in urban districts report that physical conflicts among students are a moderate or serious problem in their school. This figure is 31 percent for non-urban schools (see Figure 5).[6]

- Half of the students from urban school districts fail to graduate on time, if at all (See Figure 3).[7]

- Low expectations have consequences: The performance of 17-year-old African-American and Hispanic students is equal to that of 13-year-old white students in every subject.[8]

Stagnant Scores

- **Mathematics:** Average 1996 NAEP scores for 17-year-olds are not significantly different than they were in 1973.

- **Writing:** Average 1996 NAEP scores among 17-year-olds are lower than they were in 1984, a year after *A Nation at Risk* was released.

- **Reading:** The average score of 17-year-olds in 1996 is not significantly different than their counterparts in 1971.

Unprepared to Compete in a Global Marketplace:

- Data from the Third International Mathematics and Science Study (TIMSS) suggest that the "relative international standing" of U.S. students declines as they reach higher grades in school.[9]

---

[4] National Center for Education Statistics, *1992 National Adult Literacy Survey*. See: http://nces.ed.gov/nadlits/overview.html

[5] National Center for Education Statistics, *Literacy Behind Prison Walls: Profiles of the Prison Population from the National Adult Literacy Survey*, 1992.

[6] "Quality Counts 1998: The Urban Challenge" *Education Week*, January 8, 1998. Analysis based on the U.S. Department of Education's Common Core of Data. See: *http://www.edweek.com/sreports/qc98/*

[7] *Ibid.*

[8] Diane Ravitch, "Student Performance Today," *Policy Brief* No. 23, Brookings Institution, September 1997.

[9] *Pursuing Excellence: Initial Findings from the Third International Math and Science Study*, National Center for Education Statistics, February 24, 1998. *http://nces.ed.gov/timss*.

- U.S. 12th graders only outperformed two out of 21 nations in mathematics.[10]

- Public institutions of higher education annually spend $1 billion on remedial education.[11] Nearly 30 percent of first-time college freshmen enroll in at least one remedial course and 80 percent of all public, four-year universities offered remedial courses.[12]

- In 1995, private-sector and federal employers spent a combined $55.3 billion to provide training in basic academic skills.[13] According to U.S. manufacturers, 40 percent of all 17-year-olds do not have the math skills and 60 percent lack the reading skills to hold down a production job at a manufacturing company.[14]

Academic Improvement Since *A Nation at Risk*: Not Exactly the S&P 500

Unlike the explosive growth in the stock market the nation has experienced since the early 1980s, the pace of academic improvement since 1983 has been painstakingly slow, and numerous indicators are showing continued signs of stagnation or decline.

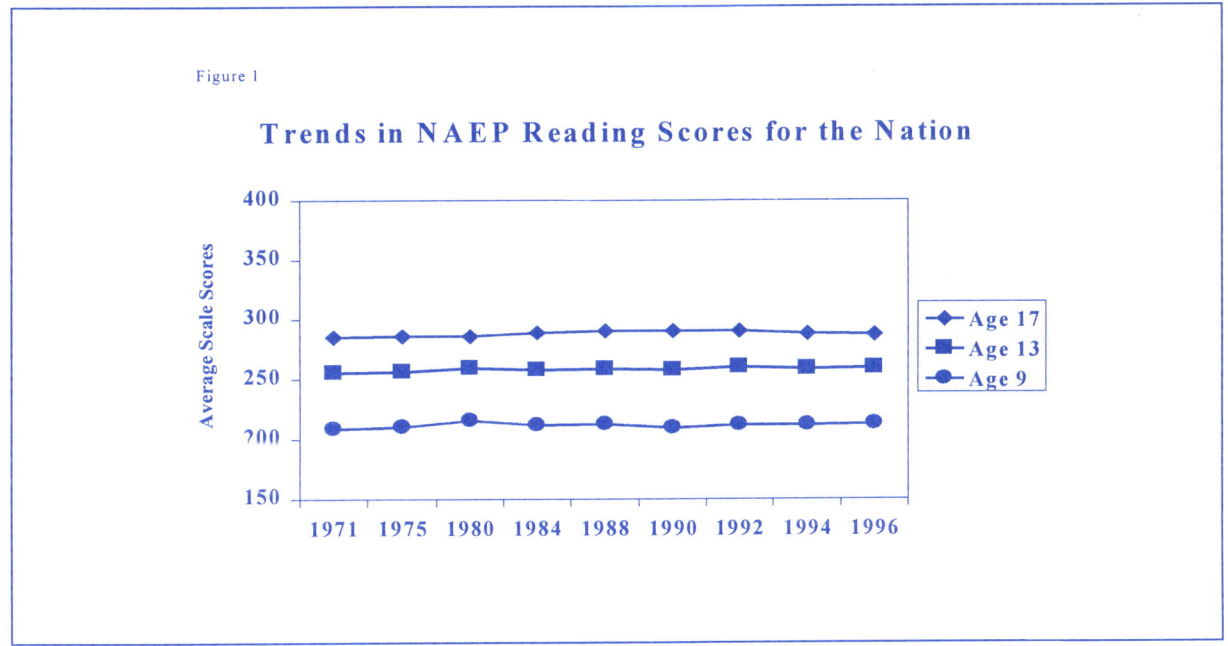

Figure 1

Trends in NAEP Reading Scores for the Nation

While math scores have improved slightly over the past 15 years, reading scores have not (Figures 1 and 2). In 1994, 30 percent of fourth graders, 30 percent of eighth-graders and 36

---

[10] *Ibid.*
[11] David W. Breneman, "The Extent and Cost of Remediation in Higher Education," *Brookings Papers on Education Policy*, (Washington, D.C.: The Brookings Institution, April 1998).
[12] *Ibid.*
[13] Carl Horowitz, "When Firms Are Schoolhouses," *Investors Business Daily*, April 29, 1997, p. A1.
[14] *Education and Training for America's Future*, (Washington, D.C.: National Association of Manufacturers, January 1998).

percent of 12th-graders attained the *Proficient* level in reading or higher. Only three to seven percent reached the *Advanced* level.[15]

Figure 2

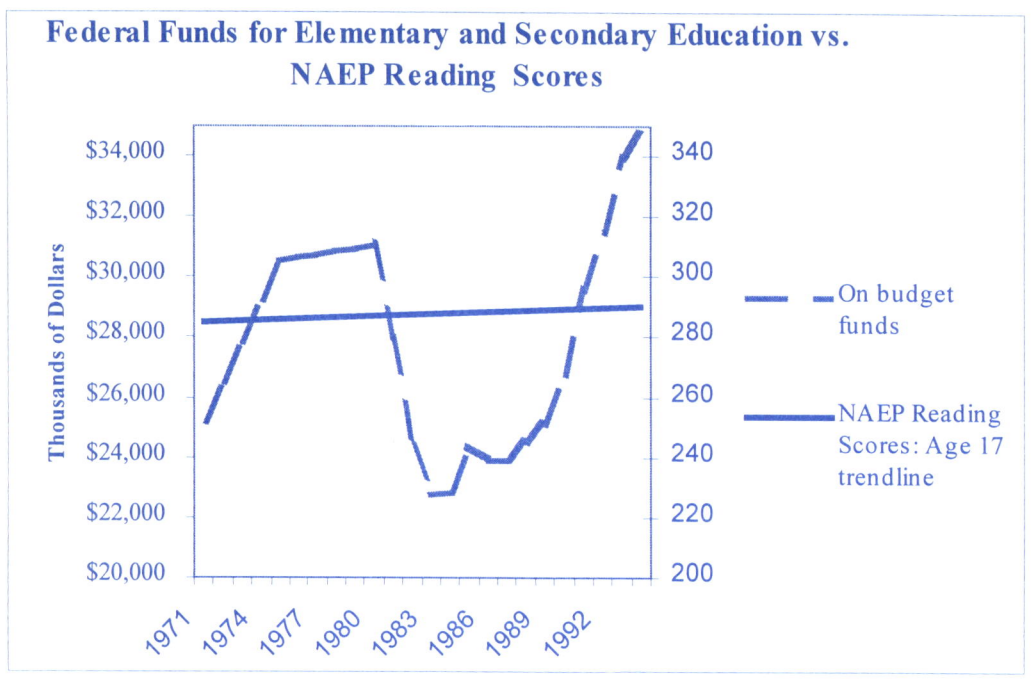

Source: U.S. Department of Education; National Center for Education Statistic, *NAEP 1994 Reading Report Card for the Nation and the States*, U.S. Department of Education, March 1996.

Impoverished Outcomes: Urban Education

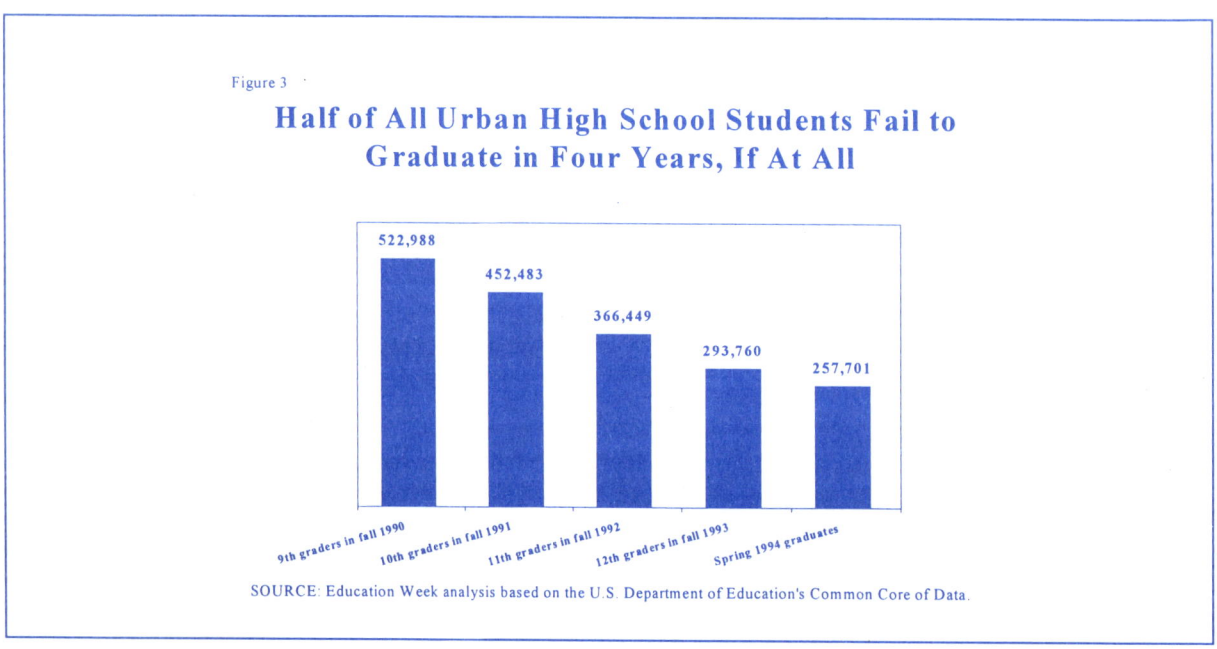

---

[15] *NAEP 1994 Reading Report Card: Findings from the National Assessment of Educational Progress, Office of Educational Research and Improvement*, U.S. Department of Education, March 1996.

This stagnation and mediocrity is magnified within urban and high-poverty areas where many obstacles exist to running successful schools. There have been repeated studies showing that students in high-poverty urban settings are falling even further behind. For example, in the District of Columbia Public School System during the 1996-97 school year:[16]

- 33 percent of third-graders scored below the basic level in reading and math;
- 72 percent of eighth-graders scored below basic in math;
- Only 53 percent of the students entering D.C. high schools in ninth grade remained in the system to graduate four years later.

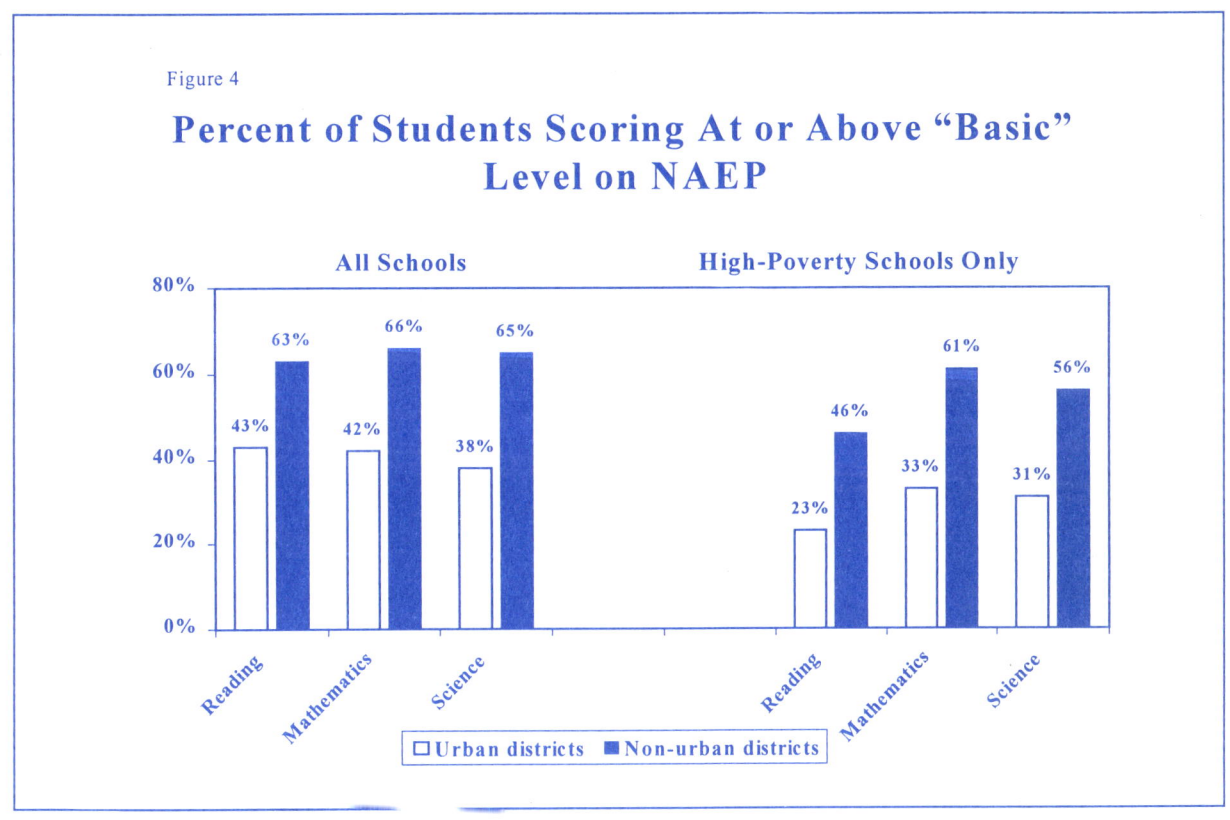

Figure 4
Percent of Students Scoring At or Above "Basic" Level on NAEP

---

[16] Committee on Education and the Workforce, *Hearing on What Works and What's Wasted in the DC School System*, May 1, 1997.

Across the country, urban schools are producing too many students who lack the skills they need to succeed. While there are many notable exceptions, students in these schools generally learn less, and in settings that are more violent and generally less conducive to learning than suburban or rural schools. Many cities risk losing yet another generation of children to mediocrity, poverty and violence because their schools have not been held accountable for graduating their students with skills and a meaningful diploma.

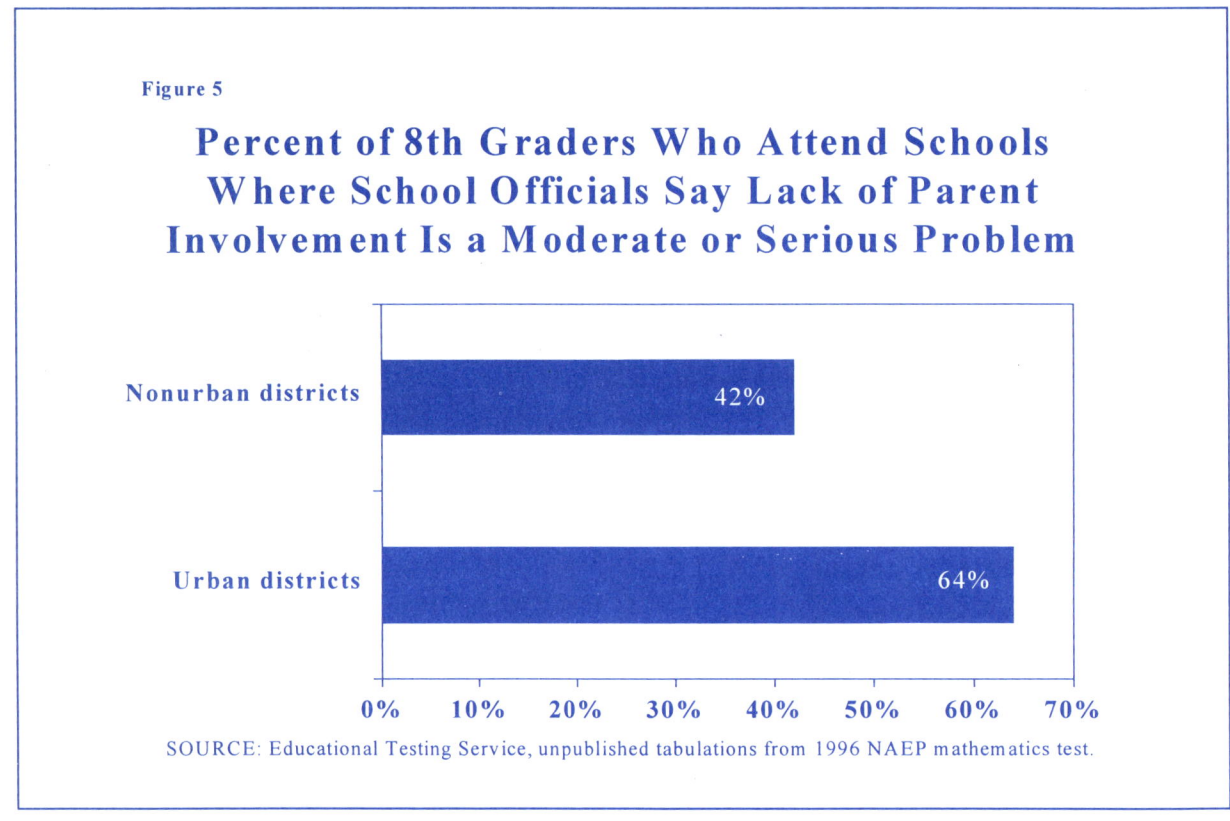

Falling Behind in the Global Marketplace

Compounding concerns about stagnating scores is the repeated poor performance of U.S. students in international comparisons. The recent Third International Mathematics and Science Study (TIMSS), provides an in-depth analysis of how the United States ranks globally at the fourth, eighth and twelfth grade achievement levels.[17]

12th Grade: U.S. Lags Behind in Math and Science
The Third Annual International Math and Science Study (TIMSS)

NATIONS WITH AVERAGE SCORES SIGNIFICANTLY HIGHER THAN THE U.S.	
NATION	AVERAGE
(NETHERLANDS)	560
SWEDEN	552
(DENMARK)	547
SWITZERLAND	540
(ICELAND)	534
(NORWAY)	528
(FRANCE)	523
NEW ZEALAND	522
(AUSTRALIA)	522
(CANADA)	519
(AUSTRIA)	518
(SLOVENIA)	512
(GERMANY)	495
HUNGARY	483

NATIONS WITH AVERAGE SCORES NOT SIGNIFICANTLY DIFFERENT FROM THE U.S.	
NATION	AVERAGE
(ITALY)	476
(RUSSIAN FEDERATION)	471
(LITHUANIA)	469
CZECH REPUBLIC	466
(UNITED STATES)	**461**

NATIONS WITH AVERAGE SCORES SIGNIFICANTLY LOWER THAN THE U.S.	
NATION	AVERAGE
(CYPRUS)	446
(SOUTH AFRICA)	356

INTERNATIONAL AVERAGE = 500

NOTE: Nations not meeting international sampling and other guidelines are shown in parentheses.

SOURCE: Mullis et al. (1998). *Mathematics and Science Achievement in the Final Year of Secondary School.* Table 2.1. Chestnut Hill. MA: Boston College.

The TIMSS study shows that in the eighth grade, 20 countries outperformed U.S. students in both math and science. This places the U.S. ahead of only seven countries – Iran, Kuwait, Columbia, South Africa, Cyprus, Portugal, and Lithuania. U.S. 12th-graders scored below the international average and among the lowest of the 21 TIMSS nations in both mathematics and science general knowledge in the final year of secondary school, only outscoring Cyprus and South Africa.

The scores of America's best and brightest in math and science do not improve this dismal picture. The performance of U.S. twelfth-grade advanced mathematics students was among the lowest of the 16 TIMSS nations. Eleven nations outperformed the United States, while our scores were not significantly different from those of four other nations. *Not one single country scored below the United States on the assessment of advanced mathematics.*

Interestingly, students from the U.S. do not fare so poorly in the earlier years, and only begin to fall behind toward their middle-school years (Figure 6). The study found that when comparing

---

[17] The Third International Mathematics and Science Study (TIMSS) represents the most extensive investigation of mathematics and science education ever conducted. The study is sponsored by the International Association for the Evaluation of Educational Achievement, and is funded by the National Science Foundation and the National Center for Education Statistics.

fourth-grade achievement levels to their international counterparts, the United States fared very well. U.S. students performed above the international mean in both math and science. In science, U.S. students in the fourth grade were out-performed by only one country – Korea.

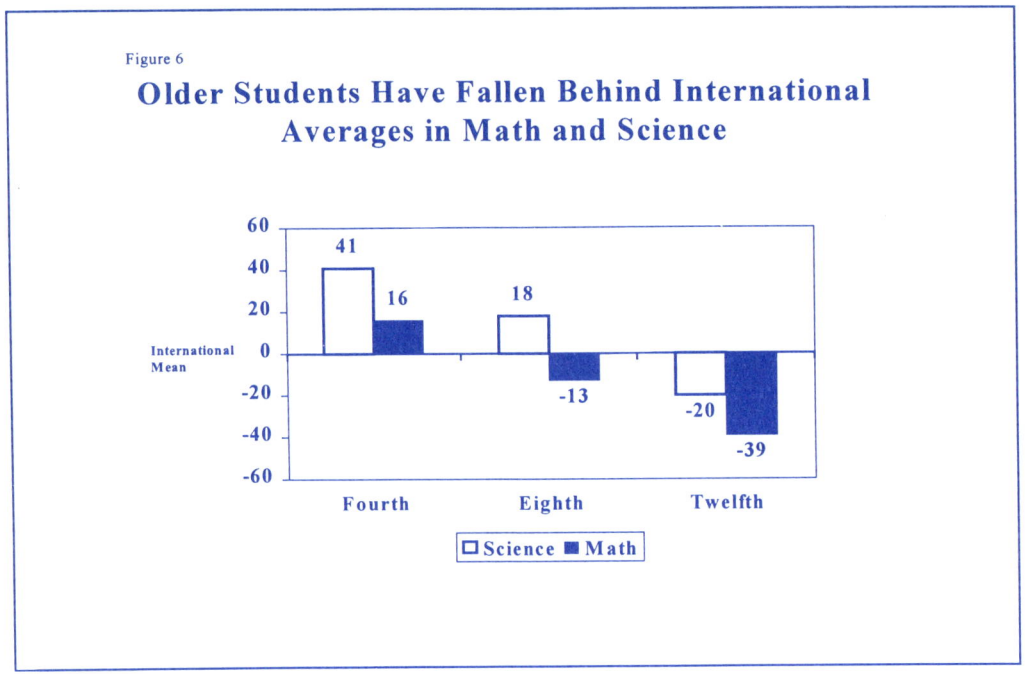

The factors behind the declining international performance of U.S. students must be addressed. In today's global economy, such results suggest that our students are competitive in the earlier grades, but when they enter the job market, they are at a serious competitive disadvantage. Furthermore, these scores only provide part of the picture. International comparisons center on mean averages and tend to mask the extent of dismal scores of those students that fall below the mean within each country.

Birth of the "Crossroads Project"

When Congressman Hoekstra became Chairman of the Subcommittee on Oversight and Investigations in 1994, he immediately directed the Subcommittee to begin a review of successful schools and school systems around the country in order to guide the Committee's understanding of what is working in education. By establishing successful schools as the standard, the Subcommittee could then review what factors led to their success, and analyze to what extent federal education policy contributed or detracted from those factors.

GAO Report on Best Practices

To this end, Mr. Hoekstra's first step as Chairman of the Subcommittee was to commission a study by the General Accounting Office (GAO) to compile a list of schools that performed exceptionally well. Chairman Hoekstra then requested that the GAO identify, even if only in a rudimentary way, the key factors or practices that were shared by each. The result was striking. Success in these institutions was not based on educational levels of teachers, the socioeconomic status of its students, or on the amount of money that was invested by the school district. Instead, the key shared components of successful schools were found to include the following:

- A well-defined mission focused on academics;
- An environment that encourages parental involvement and collaboration with staff;
- School autonomy;
- Rigorous and well-focused curricula;
- Effective and engaging instruction.[18]

Finding Success in Chicago

Armed with this information, in May 1995 Chairman Hoekstra decided to hold a field hearing in Chicago, IL, home to one of the most troubled school districts in the country. His goal was to gather testimony, to visit schools that were beating the odds by performing at exceptional levels, and to look for evidence of key success factors identified in the GAO report.

The Subcommittee visited a private elementary school, Our Lady of the Gardens, situated in a housing project on the far south side of Chicago. Here, in the middle of a community riddled by violence, poverty and decay, where public schools had a dropout rate approaching 60 percent, the Subcommittee saw a school whose graduates attended college at a rate exceeding 95 percent. The contrast was stunning. To what did the principal attribute her success? Confirming the findings of the GAO report on best practices, the principal credited strong parental involvement, autonomous control, and an emphasis on basic academics.

Later that same day, the Subcommittee toured and held a hearing at Washington Irving Elementary School, a public school in a low-income area just south of the Eisenhower Expressway. This school, which once performed well below average, now led the city in academic achievement. A tour of the school revealed teachers leading creative classroom projects – utilizing resources not typically seen in large, urban schools, students actively involved in the lessons they were being taught, and parents helping in many, if not most, of the classrooms visited by the Subcommittee. To what did the principal attribute her success? She took control of her school's budget, driving resources away from bureaucracies and into her classrooms. She pressured poor teachers to move out of the school, and unilaterally ended social

---

[18] U.S. General Accounting Office, *Schools and Workplaces: An Overview of Successful and Unsuccessful Practices,* GAO/PEMD-95-28, August, 1995, p. 3.

promotion. Today in her school, a student will not graduate beyond the eighth grade unless he or she can read and perform math at an eighth-grade level.[19]

The hearing held by the Subcommittee that day included many similar success stories – all with the same basic underlying themes behind their success: active parental involvement, an emphasis on basic academics, and a determination to focus limited resources on classroom needs.[20]

THE FEDERAL ROLE IN EDUCATION: Bureaucracy vs. Children

Considering the themes that were emerging as the keys to successful schools, Chairman Hoekstra asked the Subcommittee to determine the full scope of federal education spending to determine to what extent these four basic principles were taken into consideration in the development and implementation of federal education policy.

What the Subcommittee has found in federal education programs is an abysmal, bureaucratic response to the serious education problems of our nation. Indeed, findings produced by the Crossroads project have found that:

- **Federal education programs lack evidence of effectiveness;**
- **Federal education programs are often inefficient and duplicative.**

Just How Large is the Federal Education Bureaucracy?

The first step in this process was to determine how many federal education programs currently exist. The Subcommittee soon learned that this was not an easy question to answer. In fact, in a hearing before this Committee, Secretary of Education Richard Riley admitted that he did not know exactly how many federal education programs exist.

Hoekstra: How many education programs do you estimate that we have throughout the Federal government?

Riley: We have – what is the page? It's around 200. I've got it here. One thing that I do think is misleading is to talk about 760 –

Hoekstra: Well, how many do you think there are?

Riley: We have – I've got a page here with it.

Hoekstra: Just the Department of Education alone or is this including all other agencies?

---

[19] Committee on Economic and Educational Opportunities, Subcommittee on Oversight and Investigations, *Hearing on Leading Edge Practices in Education*, Chicago, IL, May 19, 1995, No. 104-38.
[32] *Ibid.*

Riley: It's just a couple less than 200.

Hoekstra: Is this just the Department of Education?

Riley: Just the Department of Education.

Hoekstra: How about including other agencies and those kinds of things?

Riley: Well, that's where I was going to get into the 760.

Hoekstra: I'm not talking about 760. I'm talking about your analysis of how many you think there are, including the other agencies.

Riley: You mean education programs?

Hoekstra: Yes, K-12, higher ed.

Riley: Well, I haven't analyzed any reference to something that might touch on that in some indirect way, but as far as I know, those programs are really in our department, generally, unless you're talking about the Indian programs under Interior, and of course, you've got Defense Department programs under Defense.

760 Federal Education Programs...and Counting

Because neither the U.S. Department of Education nor any other federal agency was able to provide accurate information concerning the number of federal education programs, the Subcommittee decided to compile the list independently. The result was the most comprehensive list of federal education programs that had ever been compiled.

During 1995 and 1996, the Committee assembled this list using information provided by the Office of Management and Budget's (OMB's) Catalog of Federal Domestic Assistance (CFDA). The Congressional Research Service (CRS) then identified more than 100 additional programs that OMB did not include under its definition of "Educational Programs" in the CFDA. The initial list amounted to 760 federal education programs that spanned 39 separate agencies, boards, and commissions at the cost about $100 billion (1995 figures).

Next, the Committee contacted the 39 agencies and requested verification that the programs were within their jurisdiction. If the programs were correctly identified, the agencies were asked to provide essential information on each program in order to allow the Committee to properly oversee the programs. Agencies were also asked to submit additional program names if applicable. Since February 1996, the federal agencies have added more than 100 programs to the original list of 760.

Working with the information from the CFDA, CRS, and federal agencies, the Committee spent months updating the list—adding fiscal year 1997 funding information and analyzing the programs. Approximately 100 programs were removed from the list because they were either repealed, or because they were only marginally "educational" despite having been defined as such by OMB. However, each and every program, whether funded or unfunded, is listed as an active federal program by the Office of Management and Budget. Thus, schools and universities must sift through these programs in their search for federal funds, whether or not they are actually funded.

Around the same time that the Subcommittee was compiling its list of 760 federal education programs, the Subcommittee learned that the Education Funding Research Council, a private organization that identifies potential sources of funds for local school districts, produces the *Guide to Federal Funding for Education*. The company promises to steer its subscribers to "a wide range of Federal programs," and offers these subscribers timely updates on "500 education programs." More recently, the *Aid for Education Report* published by CD Publications advertised that "huge sums are available…in the federal government alone, there are nearly 800 different education programs that receive authorization totaling almost a hundred billion dollars." In short, the leviathan of federal education programs has actually led to a cottage industry in selling information on program descriptions, application deadlines and filing instructions for each of the myriad of federal education programs.

On May 8, 1997, the list was published and a number of Members of Congress, including the Speaker of the House, sent a letter to the President, soliciting his support for the on-going task of evaluating the federal role in education. Even though the Secretary received a list of actual education programs, verified by both CRS and OMB, nevertheless on July 14, 1997, Secretary Riley stated by letter on behalf of the President that the list of 760 federal education programs is "significantly overstated."

Table 2
1997 Federal Education Spending: Departments, Programs and Funding

Department	Number of Programs	Federal Dollars
Appalachian Regional Commission	2	$2,000,000
Barry Goldwater Scholarship Program	1	$2,900,000
Christopher Columbus Fellowship Program	1	$0.00
Corporation for National Service	11	$501,130,000
Department of Education	307	$59,045,043,938
Department of Commerce	20	$156,455,000
Department of Defense	15	$2,815,320,854
Department of Energy	22	$36,700,000
Department of Health and Human Services	172	$8,661,006,166
Department of the Treasury	1	$11,000,000
Department of Interior	27	$555,565,000
Department of Housing and Urban Development	9	$81,800,000
Department of Justice	21	$755,447,149
Department of Labor	21	$5,474,039,000
Department of Transportation	19	$121,672,000
Department of Veterans' Affairs	6	$1,436,074,000
Environmental Protection Agency	4	$11,103,800
Federal Emergency Management Administration	6	$118,512,000
General Services Administration	1	$0.00
Government Printing Office	2	$24,756,000
Harry Truman Scholarship Foundation	1	$3,187,000
James Madison Memorial Fellowship Program	1	$2,000,000
Library of Congress	5	$194,822,103
National Aeronautics and Space Administration	12	$153,300,000
National Archives	2	$5,000,000
National Institute for Literacy	1	$4,491,000
National Council on Disability	1	$200,000
National Endowment for the Arts/Humanities	13	$103,219,000
National Science Foundation	15	$2,939,230,000
Nuclear Regulatory Commission	3	$6,944,000
National Gallery of Art	1	$750,000
Office of Personnel Management	1	$0.00
Small Business Administration	2	$73,540,000
Smithsonian	14	$3,276,000
State Department	1	$0.00
United States Information Agency	8	$125,558,000
United States Institute for Peace	4	$3,371,000
United Stated Department of Agriculture	33	$13,339,630,410
US Agency for International Development	1	$14,600,000
Social Security Administration	1	$85,700,000

Total Number of Programs: 788   **Total Funding: $96,869,343,420.00**

Note: This table includes all authorized programs regardless of funding, as well as off-budget spending (such as student lending programs).
See also: U.S. Department of Education, *Digest of Education Statistics, 1997*, Tables 358-9.

Figure 7: The Current Federal Role in Education

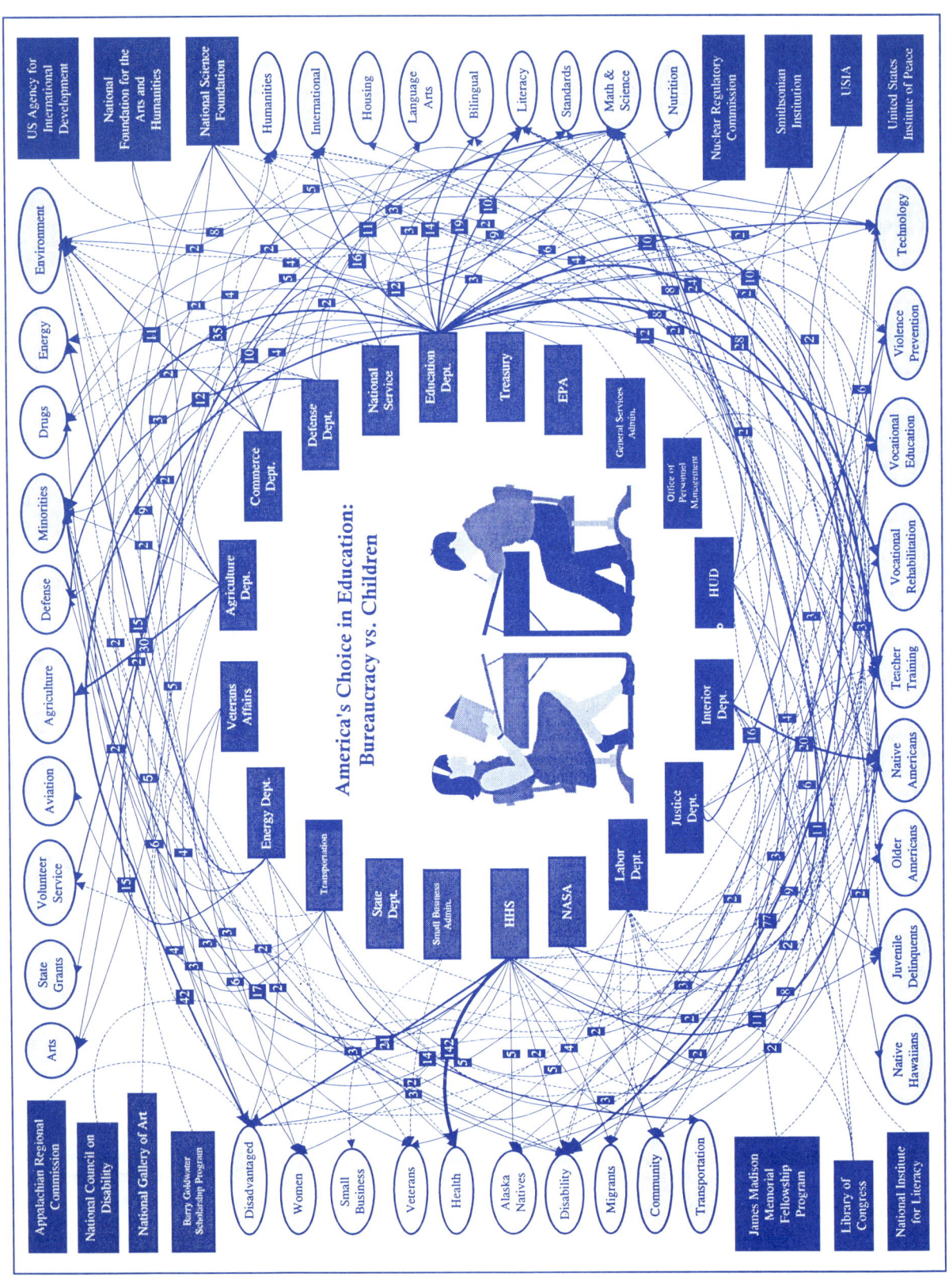

It Takes a Village to Complete the Paperwork

One of the main problems with delivering federal education aid to states and communities through such a vast array of programs is the added cost in paperwork and personnel necessary to apply for and to keep track of the operations of each of these programs. Many of the costs are hidden in the burdens placed on teachers and administrators in time and money to complete federal forms for this multitude of overlapping federal programs.

Ohio: 50 percent of Paperwork for Six Percent of Funds

In 1996 Governor Voinovich of Ohio noted that local schools in his state had to submit as many as 170 federal reports totaling more than 700 pages during a single year. This report also noted that more than 50 percent of the paperwork required by a local school in Ohio is a result of federal programs - this despite the fact that the federal government accounts for only 6 percent of Ohio's educational spending.[21]

The Subcommittee has attempted to quantify the number of pages required by recipients of federal funds in order to qualify for assistance. Without fully accounting for all the attachments and supplemental submissions required with each application, the Subcommittee counted more than 20,000 pages of applications.

25,000 Paperwork Employees

So how much time is spent completing this paperwork? In the recently released strategic plan of the Department of Education, the administration highlights the success of the Department in reducing paperwork burdens by an estimated 10 percent – which according to their own estimate accounts for 5.4 million man hours in FY 1997.[22] If this statistic is accurate, it would mean that the Department of Education is still requiring nearly 50 million hours worth of paperwork each year – or the equivalent of 25,000 employees working full-time.

A Nine-Pound Application "Birthed" in Boston

Unfortunately, even this estimate is likely to underestimate the true paperwork burden to local schools and universities across the country. According to the President of Boston University, Jon Westling, Boston University spent 14 weeks and approximately 2,700 employee hours completing the paperwork required to qualify for federal Title IV funding. They were slowed by the repeated corrections and clarifications requested by the Department. In the end, the University spent the equivalent of 1.5 personnel years compiling what turned out to be a nine-pound application. Interestingly, the Department of Education had estimated that the application should only take three hours to complete. Considering that there are 6,500

---

[21] Ohio State Legislature, Legislative Office of Education Oversight, "Public School Reporting Requirements," RR9002, October 1990.
[22] Marshall Smith, "Paper Reduction Act Accomplishments and Plans for Future," U.S. Department of Education, October 31, 1996.

institutions of higher education, the paperwork needed for Title IV alone could account for 9,700 employees each year.[23]

The "Shadow" Department of Education

The Department of Education touts that it is one of the smallest federal agencies with 4,637 employees, and that it has a relatively small administrative budget. What many people do not realize, however, is that there is nearly three times as many federally funded employees of state education agencies administering federal education programs, as there are U.S. Department of Education employees. According to GAO, there are about 13,400 FTEs (full-time equivalents) funded with federal dollars to administer these programs for state education agencies.[24]

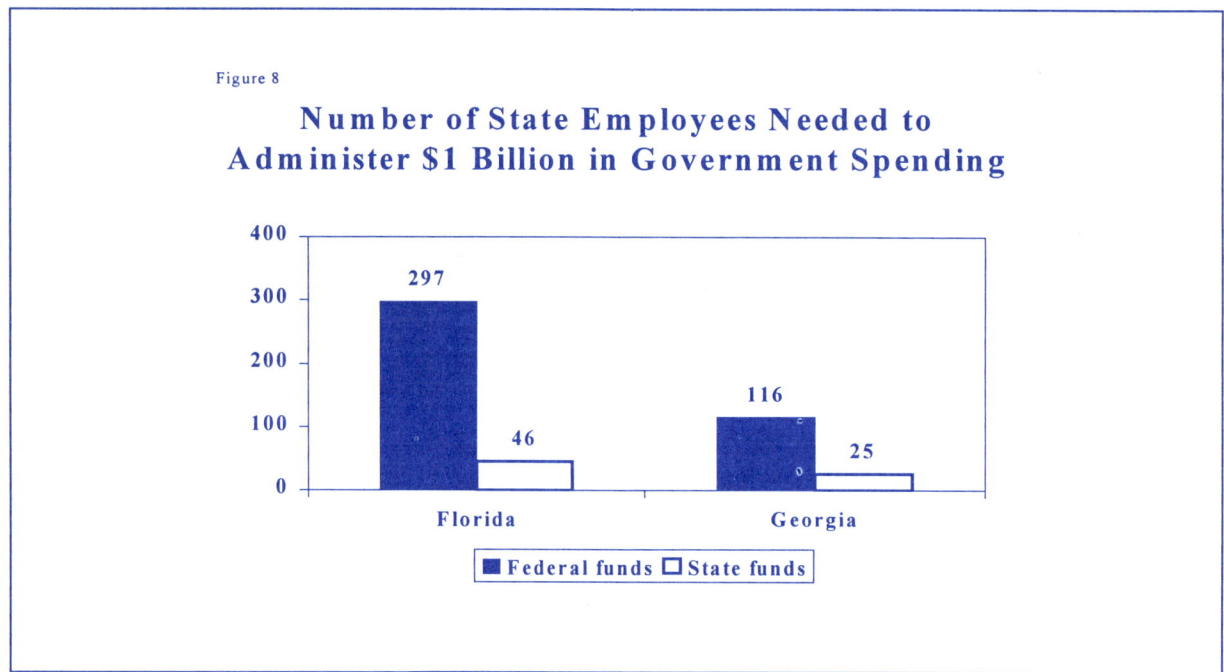

Figure 8
Number of State Employees Needed to Administer $1 Billion in Government Spending

The Department also has the lowest ratio of career civil service employees to political appointees of all the agencies - 29.7 career employees for every political appointee, 146 political appointees for an agency with about 4,600 employees. The next lowest ratio is the Agency for Housing and Urban Development (HUD), with 97.5 employees for every political appointee. What that means is that HUD only has 101 appointees for an agency of 10,400 employees - which is more than twice the size of the Education Department.[25]

Several state administrators have observed that it takes many more state employees to administer federal program dollars than state funded programs. For example, in Florida, 374 employees administer $8 billion in state funds. However, 297 state employees are required to

---

[23] Jon Westling, "Getting Government out of Higher Education," *Heritage Foundation Lecture*, May 3, 1995.
[24] U.S. General Accounting Office, *Education Finance: The Extent of Federal Funding in State Education Agencies*, GAO/HEHS-95-3, October, 1994, p. 11. The number of full-time equivalents is not necessarily the total number of employees.
[25] Congressional Research Service, based on data from the Office of Personnel Management, March 1998.

oversee only $1 billion in federal funds - six times as many per dollar. In Georgia, 229 employees administer $8.85 billion in state funds, while 93 administer $800 million in federal funds - 4.5 times as many per dollar.[26]

65 Cents on the Dollar?

A recent study found that for every tax dollar sent to Washington for elementary and secondary education, 85 cents is returned to local school districts. The remaining 15 cents is spent on bureaucracy and national and research programs of unknown effectiveness.[27] The study also found that some states receive a greater return per tax dollar than do others. Connecticut has the lowest return on its investment – only 39 cents for every tax dollar (See Table 3). The Department of Education has since released a study, which also found that about 85 cents of federal dollars reaches school districts for use in the classroom.[28] Although these studies provided information not previously available on federal education spending, they only examined what returned to school districts, still several layers of bureaucracy away from the classroom.

---

[26] Testimonies of Dr. Linda Schrenko and Frank Brogran, Committee on Education and the Workforce, *Hearing on H.R. 3248,"The Dollars to the Classroom Act,"* U.S. House of Representatives, May 5, 1998.
[27] Christine L. Olson, *U.S. Department of Education Financing of Elementary and Secondary Education: Where the Money Goes*, (Washington, DC: The Heritage Foundation), December 30, 1996; Subcommittee on Oversight and Investigations, *Dollars to the Classroom,* May 8, 1997, No. 105-27.
[28] U.S. Department of Education, Planning and Evaluation Service, *The Use of Federal Education Funds for Administrative Costs*, 1998, p. 28.

Table 3

For Every Dollar Sent to Washington for Department of Education Elementary and Secondary Education Programs, Only 85 Cents is Received by Local Education Agencies FY 1993

States	Amount Received Per Individual Tax Dollar
Alabama	$1.29
Alaska	$3.12
Arizona	$1.42
Arkansas	$1.49
California	$0.83
Colorado	$0.58
Connecticut	$0.39
Delaware	$0.78
District of Columbia*	$1.10
Florida	$0.80
Georgia	$0.85
Hawaii*	$1.05
Idaho	$1.11
Illinois	$0.64
Indiana	$0.72
Iowa	$0.76
Kansas	$0.73
Kentucky	$1.31
Louisiana	$1.66
Maine	$1.17
Maryland	$0.56
Massachusetts	$0.58
Michigan	$0.90
Minnesota	$0.61
Mississippi	$2.41
Missouri	$0.79
Montana	$2.13
Nebraska	$0.89
Nevada	$0.39
New Hampshire	$0.47
New Jersey	$0.53
New Mexico	$2.34
New York	$0.79
North Carolina	$0.83
North Dakota	$1.75
Ohio	$0.81
Oklahoma	$1.54
Oregon	$0.78
Pennsylvania	$0.78
Rhode Island	$0.86
South Carolina	$1.24
South Dakota	$1.66
Tennessee	$0.88
Texas	$1.03
Utah	$1.06
Vermont	$1.04
Virginia	$0.68
Washington	$0.64
West Virginia	$1.61
Wisconsin	$0.82
Wyoming	$1.28
50 States, D.C.	$0.85

Source: Christine L. Olson, *U.S. Department of Education Financing of Elementary and Secondary Education: Where the Money Goes*, (Washington, DC: The Heritage Foundation), December 30, 1996.

To date, no studies exist to enable us to determine what portion of federal education dollars reach the classroom nationwide, or what schools and state education agencies must spend to apply for education dollars and comply with their requirements. However, audits of school district spending indicate just how little in general reaches the classroom. A recent audit of the New York City School District found that only 43 percent of the district's total funds were spent on direct classroom expenditures.[29] Given the 48.6 million paperwork hours required to receive federal education dollars and the school district bureaucracies funds must pass through to reach the classroom, it is not unreasonable to assume that another 20-15 cents spent outside the classroom. This would mean a <u>net return</u> of 65-70 cents to the classroom.

For example, Dr. Charles Garris, the superintendent of the small Unionville-Chadds Ford School District in eastern Pennsylvania, testified that he has been questioning whether applying for federal funds is worth the expense. He did the math to determine what he had spent to apply for federal funds for the 1997-98 school year. Before the end of the year he had spent over $2,400, which is 13 percent of the $21,796 he expects to receive from the federal government. Moreover, based on past years, he can expect to spend at least another 25 percent of his allotment on administration before it reaches classrooms because of federal requirements. As a result, Dr. Garris has decided that it is no longer cost effective even to apply for certain programs.

Enough is Enough

To determine what administrators at the local level thought of federal programs, the Subcommittee sent out surveys to local school superintendents from 10 states to solicit their input on a variety of issues (See Appendix B). One area about which they were questioned concerned their view of the paperwork burden that accompanies federal education funding. One superintendent, feeling that the survey we sent was one too many forms for him to complete wrote,

> *We have too much paperwork and too many forms to fill out, and then we receive this...the purpose of federal education programs should be to help children...I think your Committee should work on these things.*

While most of the questions posed in the survey invoked varied responses, the concern over the paperwork burden was unanimous. The repeated theme was that paperwork reduction should be a top priority of the administration and the Congress.

---

[29] Jacques Steinberg, "NYC School System Budget Analysis Shows 43% Goes to Classroom," *The New York Times*, November 21, 1996. See also: Speakman, Cooper, Sampiere, May, Holsomback, Glass, "Bringing Money to the Classroom: A Systemic Resource Model Applied to the New York City Public Schools," in *Where Does the Money Go? Resource Allocation in Elementary and Secondary Schools*, Lawrence O. Picus and James L. Wattenberger, eds. (Thosand Oaks, CA: Corwin Press, 1995).

The 487-Step Labyrinth: Government Attempts to Reinvent Itself

The next issue addressed by the Subcommittee was the amount of time and number of personnel required by the federal government to read, review, and file applications for federal grants. The Subcommittee found that the Department of Education's discretionary grant process lasted 26 weeks and took 487 steps from start to finish. It is unclear how many individuals are involved in each step. Even though Vice President Gore's National Performance Review discovered this long and protracted process in 1993, it was not until 1996 that the Department finally took steps to begin "streamlining" their grant review process, a process which has yet to be completed and fully implemented. After the streamlining is complete it will *only* take an average of 20 weeks and 216 steps to complete a review.[30] This is an unnecessarily complicated and burdensome process that, according to the Department, is "central to nearly all the Department's services" and is "a major function at the Department of Education."[31]

Costly Requirements and Regulations

Congress and the federal government have created many programs to improve education, but have not been able to provide funding for all of them. Consequently, states and local school districts must come up with the rest of the funds out of their education budgets to comply with federally mandated requirements. Many of these requirements regulate asbestos removal and disabled access to school buildings. One of the most contentious and costly mandates for many local school districts, however, is special education.

Twenty-three years ago in 1975, Congress passed the Individuals with Disabilities Education Act (IDEA). This historic legislation requires local school districts to provide disabled students with a "free and appropriate education," which, while bringing federal aid to disabled children also mandated that communities fund special education at much higher levels. However, when it was passed, Congress agreed to fund 40 percent of its cost. Currently it only funds 9 percent, which means that states and districts must make up the difference. Because the federal government has not met its obligation to states and schools, there are fewer funds available to meet the unique needs and priorities of local schools.

Scores of Programs for Every Problem

A reasonable justification for this myriad of federal education programs could be that there are 760 separate and distinct problems, and that each program addresses one of them. Unfortunately, this is not the case. After identifying each and every education program scattered throughout the federal government, the Subcommittee categorized the programs according to their mission and by the services they provide. The Subcommittee then separated each category into more specific subject categories and then listed them according to the population they were intended to serve.

---

[30] U.S. Department of Education Report, "A Redesigned Discretionary Grant Process" - Vice President Gore's National Performance Review 1995.
[31] *Ibid.*

The Subcommittee found an incredible overlap and duplication in the services and populations covered by separate federal education programs. For example, the Subcommittee found nine art programs, 11 drug education programs, 14 literacy programs, 22 violence prevention programs and 63 math and science programs. GAO has found more than 127 programs targeting at-risk and delinquent youth. And according to GAO, "multiple programs dispersed among several agencies creates the potential for inefficient services and ineffective use of funds." (See Figure 9)[32]

Figure 9: Three Target Groups Served by Multiple Programs and Agencies[33]

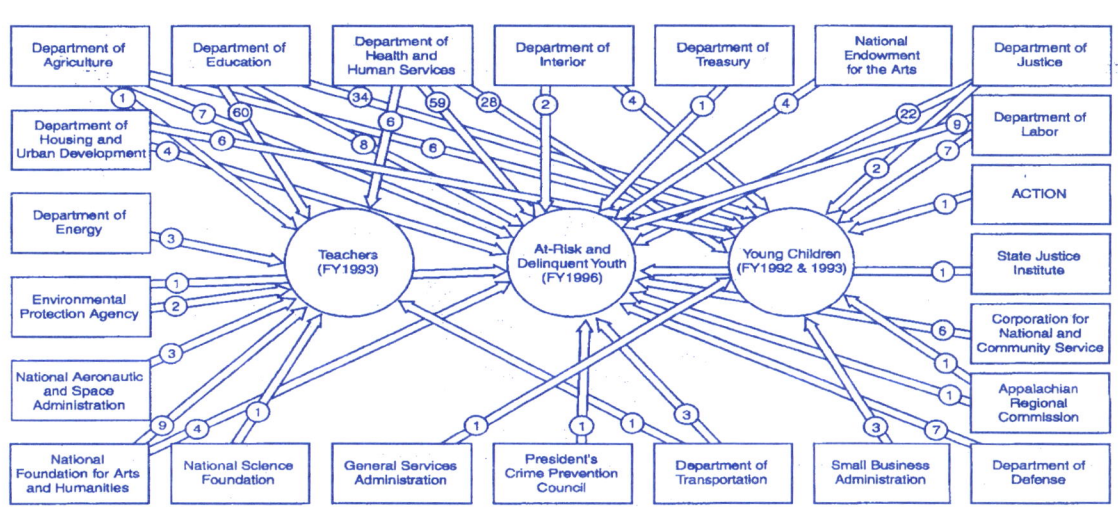

Additional evidence of duplication and overlap is evident in that many cabinet agencies have their own education offices. For example, despite the existence of 63 math and science programs, the Department of Energy has a division devoted to "Education in Science, Technology, Engineering and Math."[34] This division provides curriculum support, teacher training and other scientific information. The Department recently announced the creation of a new "education task force" devoted to determine how it can best enhance science, math and technology education, as well as providing schools with access to its scientific, technological and supercomputing resources.

In addition to the Department of Energy's K-12 education programs, there are many other examples of overlapping programs between agencies, and although attempts have recently been made to consolidate some duplicative programs, much work remains to be done.

---

[32] U.S. General Accounting Office, *Safe and Drug-Free Schools: Balancing Accountability with State and Local Flexibility,* GAO/HEHS-98-3, p. 8.
[33] U.S. General Accounting Office, *Federal Education Funding: Multiple Programs and Lack of Data Raise Efficiency and Effectiveness Concerns,* GAO/HEHS-98-46, p. 8.
[34] The Energy Department's Education Community Web site, *http://www.sandia.gov/ESTEEM/home.html*

Baywatch and Jerry Springer: Your Tax Dollars at Work

The Department of Education's Office of Special Education and Rehabilitative Services, Media and Captioning Services provides deaf and visually impaired individuals with access to films, videos, and television programs, many of which are of dubious cultural or educational merit. The objective of this program is supposedly to promote the general welfare of the deaf and hard-of-hearing by bringing to those individuals films, videos and television programs that play an important part in the general cultural advancement of hearing individuals. According to the Department, if it's on television, "it's part of the culture," says Ernest Hairston, an associate director in the Education Department's office of special education programs.[35]

Closed captioning is provided for "diverse" programs such as:
- *Baywatch*
- *Ricki Lake*
- *The Montel Williams Show*
- *Jerry Springer*

A special program is dedicated to closed captioning major sports programs.[36]

Some of the federally funded captioned shows are far from being "family television." For example, the *Jerry Springer* show issues a "strong advisory" prior to the show urging parents not to let their children watch it. Recent episodes include "Stripper Wars," "I Have a Bizarre Sex Life," and "You Can't Have My Man." The show is a huge hit with young people, according to the ratings, which has caused at least one NBC affiliate to pull the show out of concern for "youth viewership" and alleged outbreaks of school fights inspired by the show.[37]

By funding captioning for these programs - funding which could easily be provided by the television industry or other commercial enterprises - the federal government is demonstrating to the American people just how far away it is from supporting what works and identifying federal education priorities.

On the Playground with the Federal Government

The federal government funds hundreds of research projects at universities and private organizations around the country. One example of such a program, described as a "school improvement program" by the Department of Education, is the Women's Education Equity program. According to GAO, this program only sends 17 percent of its funds to school districts.

Over the last 22 years over the program's existence, the GAO has found "little evidence of [the program's] effectiveness in eliminating sex bias in education." It described the program as

---

[35] Steven Drummond, "Tabloid TV, Courtesy Of The Education Department," *Teacher Magazine*, April, 1998.
[36] U.S. Department of Education, Office of Special Education Programs, "Captioned Films, Television, Descriptive Video, & Educational Media for Individuals with Disabilities," 1996.
[37] Maria Glod, "'Springer' Mania: Too Hot for Parents and Teachers!," *The Washington Post,* April 27, 1998, p. A1.

one "with no director, with a staff of one and one-quarter persons in two different offices of the Department… with too many resources [going] for direct services to small numbers of persons."[38] In 1996 its grantees included a project called "Gender Based Teasing and Bullying in Grades K-5" which examines teasing and bullying as antecedents to adolescent sexual harassment.

In addition, recent statistics do not back allegations of severe sex bias in education. The latest math and science test scores indicate girls have virtually caught up in math and closed the gap in science, and for two decades girls have outperformed boys in NAEP reading scores.[39] According to the Census Bureau, recent college completion rates of students ages 25 to 29 show that the proportion of women completing college has surpassed that of men: 29.3 percent of women completed college, as compared to 26.3 percent of men.

Other "Educational" Publications from the Department of Education

- **CARTOONS** – "The Ninjas, the X-Men, and the Ladies: Playing with Power and Identity in an Urban Primary School": 25 pages;
- **BAKERY INDUSTRY** – "Lesson Plans Prepared for Carr Grocery Employees" (The lessons focus on topics from the workplace in the following areas: bakery, cake orders, courtesy clerk, and sushi bar): 96 pages;
- **FIFTH GRADE PIPEFITTERS:** "Building Workplace Vocabulary for Pipefitters: Compound Words": 27 pages;
- **CEMENT INDUSTRY** - "A Concrete Experience. A Curriculum Developed for the Cement Industry": 109 pages;
- **FEDERAL SCOUTS**: *Planning a Class Camping Trip*: 14 pages;
- **DONNA REED**: *Channeling Your Donna Reed Syndrome*. A manual on stress management for the workplace: 20 pages.

Federally Funded "Holiday Awareness"

The Safe and Drug-Free Schools program is an example of a program designed to address a very real problem, but with a one-size-fits all solution that in the end accomplishes little. The program sends funds to the majority of school districts in the country, only targeting 30 percent to areas based on need. School districts often lack the funds to supplement the federal funding and implement more expensive, research based programs. Consequently, the majority of funds are used for staff training and technical assistance.[40]

Dr. Lawrence Sherman, a witness at a Crossroads hearing examining federal drug prevention programs, summarized for the subcommittee the findings contained his 655 page report on drug prevention programs. He and his University of Maryland colleagues determined that:

---

[38] U.S. General Accounting Office, *Women's Educational Equity Act: A Review of Program Goals and Strategies Needed,* GAO/PEMD-95-6, November, 1994, p. 4.
[39] See: Barabara Vobjeda and Linda Perlstein, "Girls Close Gender Gap in Ways Welcome and Worrying," *The Washington Post*, June 17, 1998, p. A1.
[40] U.S. General Accounting Office, *Safe and Drug-Free Schools: Balancing Accountability with State and Local Flexibility,* GOA/HEHS-98-3, p. 34

> *Most crime prevention funds are being spent where they are needed least, that is, in low risk crime areas, rather than where the violence is concentrated in America. Secondly, most crime prevention programs...have not been evaluated rigorously and are not going to be unless legislative policy changes. And third...the most federal funding goes to the least effective programs.*[41]

In addition, the Subcommittee found that projects funded with federal Safe and Drug Free School Funds included the following:

- The State of Michigan spent $81,000 for giant plastic teeth and toothbrushes;[42]
- $124,000 was awarded by the U.S. Department of Education to the New Haven, Conn., Police Department to organize, among other things, a "holiday awareness project" designed to "encourage awareness of and participation in holidays and events significant to racial, religious, ethnic or sexual orientation groups;"[43]
- The Fairfax County School District in Virginia spent $181,397 to send teachers to a Maryland island resort for "training." [44]

When Safe and Drug-Free School dollars are spent on drug-prevention programs, the results have been minimal. An analysis of studies measuring the effectiveness of school-based drug prevention programs found that, based on eight "methodologically rigorous" studies, substance abuse programs like those funded by Safe and Drug-Free Schools have a very small effect on behavior.[45] A more recent study of school-based drug prevention programs funded under Safe and Drug-Free Schools found that few schools used the funds for prevention programs that have been found effective in previous research. Consequently, only a few drug prevention programs produced results, and even those effects were small.[46]

Not only has Safe and Drug-Free Schools not been found to be effective, GAO recently reported that the Safe and Drug-Free Schools program is one of 127 federal programs that target at-risk and delinquent youth, and received $2.5 billion in funding in 1995. Thirty-four provide both violence and substance prevention. The Departments of Health and Human Services,

---

[41] Statement of Dr. Lawrence W. Sherman, Department of Criminology and Criminal Justice, University of Maryland, Committee on Education and the Workforce, Subcommittee on Oversight and Investigations, *What Works? What's Wasted in Federal Drug Violence Prevention Programs?*, Washington, DC, June 24, 1997, No. 105-42, p. 25.

[42] Robert E. Peterson, "Senate Testimony and Final Drug Education Report," Michigan Office of Drug Control Policy, October 12, 1993, p. 7-8.

[43] U.S. Department of Education, Office of Elementary and Secondary Education, "Safe and Drug-Free Schools Program," FY 1996 slate.

[44] "Meetings Cost $176,000," *The Fairfax Journal*, May 1, 1995, p. A1.

[45] Susan T. Ennett, Ph.D., *et al.*, "How Effective is Drug Abuse Education? A Meta-Analysis of Project DARE Outcome Evaluations," *American Journal of Public Health*, Vol. 84, No. 9 (September 1994) p. 1394.

[46] E. Suyapa Silvia and Judy Thorne, *School-Based Drug Prevention Programs: A Longitudinal Study in Selected School Districts*, Prepared for the U.S. Department of Education, February 1997.

Education and Justice administer 48 of these programs, and the remainder are scattered in 10 other federal agencies or entities (see Figure 9).[47]

Fraught with Failure

While it is easy to laugh at the anecdotal stories of wasteful spending within many of these programs, the dismal evaluations of the overall success of these programs is not so funny.[48] Not only are many federal programs failing because the funds are allocated through such a wide array of programs, many of the individual programs within that array that have been evaluated lack evidence of success. Many of these programs were created to address particular needs, and their failure to accomplish their stated intentions simply means that taxpayer dollars are wasted.

According to GAO, "federally funded programs have historically placed a low priority on results and accountability."[49] In order to more fully document the extent to which reliable data demonstrating the effectiveness of federal programs exists, the Subcommittee compiled a summary of recent Department of Education evaluations of each of the major education programs within the Committee's jurisdiction.

What the Subcommittee found was that it is very difficult to determine whether the majority of federal education spending is doing anything to improve student achievement. It has been years since many programs have been evaluated, and often those reviews are more concerned with process - accounting for numbers of participants and educators, not whether the children are actually better off as a result of being served by a particular program. Perhaps most disturbing is that most federal education programs have **never** been evaluated to determine their impact on student outcomes.

A Complete Lack of Evidence of Effectiveness

The GAO report on best practices cited earlier also found that there are few evaluations demonstrating the effectiveness of federal education programs, and many of the studies that do exist lack the "methodological rigor" to determine effectiveness in an empirical manner. Billions of dollars are spent on programs where even the most basic information on effectiveness is lacking. GAO reported in November 1997 that "no central source of information exists about all the programs providing services to the same target groups among different agencies or about those providing a similar service to several target groups...[w]e do not know what is working and what is not in today's programs"[50]

According to the GAO, the clearest evidence about a "lack of positive effect" from federal expenditures comes from the largest, most expensive education program which has spent nearly $100 billion since 1965.[51] A recent official evaluation of this program, Aid to Disadvantaged

---

[47] U.S. General Accounting Office, *Safe and Drug-Free Schools*, p. 8.
[48] See: "Textbook Battles in the War over Federal Spending," *The Washington Times*, December 18, 1995, p. A12.
[49] U.S. General Accounting Office, *Federal Education Funding: Multiple Programs and Lack of Data Raise Efficiency and Effectiveness Concerns*, (GAO-T-HEHS-98-46) November 6, 1998, p. 17.
[50] *Ibid*, p. 13.
[51] *Ibid*, p. 11.

Children (Chapter 1, now known as Title I) determined that it did not reduce the effect of poverty on a student's achievement. The initial gap in test scores between the more disadvantaged students participating in Chapter 1 and non-participants did not narrow as a result of the more disadvantaged students participating in the special program.[52]

In 1994, Title I was changed in order to make real improvements in children's learning, and the results are not yet in on improvements in student outcomes. Its slowness to change, however, in light of a lack of evidence of effectiveness is an example of the inherent shortcomings of federally designed education programs: It takes many years' innovations and effective practices to effect change in federal laws. Allowing for experimentation, flexibility and innovation at the state and local level can facilitate this process and prevent entrenched programs from spending billions without results.

Lack of Follow-Through

Federally funded, reliable, replicable research demonstrating the effectiveness of programs and teaching methods has been relatively scarce. One instance of this type of research was Project Follow-Through, "the largest, most expensive research study in the history of education."[53] The study began in 1976 and continued through 1995, involved more than 70,000 children in more than 180 schools, and cost more than $1 billion. The purpose of the study was to determine which teaching methods could raise average performance levels of the nation's poorest schools, where test scores averaged around the 20th percentile, to that of mainstream America (the 50th, or average, percentile).

The teaching method found to have the greatest positive impact on basic reading and computation, problem solving skills, as well as self-esteem, was that of Direct Instruction. This was a controversial finding as it flew in the face of progressive educators promoting less structured, non-directive, "child-centered" education. Follow-Through found that methods of instruction that stressed "learning to learn" or "self esteem" showed either negative average effects or no average effect.[54]

Despite this massive effort which utilized empirical research to determine what works in education, the National Institute of Education, part of the U.S. Department of Education, issued a report which questioned the validity of using scientific research to measure educational outcomes:

> *The audience for Follow-Through evaluations is an audience of teachers. This audience does not need the statistical findings of experiments when deciding how to best educate children. They decide such matters on the basis of complicated public and private understandings, beliefs, motives and wishes.*

---

[52] Abt Associates, Inc., *Prospects: Final Report on Student Outcomes*, Cambridge, MA: April 1997.
[53] Bonnie Grossen, "Making Research Serve the Profession," *American Educator,* Fall 1996, p. 24.
[54] Marian Kester Coombs, "Honest Follow-Through Needed on this Project," *The Washington Times,* March 24, 1998, p. E5.

Such thinking reflected a view that regarded research-based teaching methods as irrelevant to improving student learning. According to Bonnie Grossen of the University of Oregon's National Center to Improve the Tools of Educators, this attitude "has left teachers without the tools that they need to build a sound professional knowledge base" and determine the effectiveness of innovations and avoid fads.

Even though more than $1 billion was spent to complete this study, the Department never effectively disseminated its findings. For example, one of the findings of Follow-Through was that a teaching model similar to what is known as "whole language" reading instruction was found to be an ineffective approach to use with disadvantaged students. The effective use of the data produced by Follow-Through may have prevented the "pendulum" swings from phonics to whole-language and back to phonics that have taken their toll on the reading ability of many children.[55]

Ineffective Assistance

Even programs designed to make federal programs effective do not appear to be helping their intended customers. Recognizing the complexity state and local school systems face with so many education programs with varying requirements, technical assistance is provided through what are known as Comprehensive Regional Assistance Centers (CRAC), as well as through the Regional Education Labs.

Funded at $27 million in FY 98, the CRACs assist state education agencies and local school districts in their efforts to receive federal funds and correctly implement programs. Their overall objective is "to help coordinate and integrate the implementation of the Elementary and Secondary Education Act and other federal education programs with state and local activities." Regional Labs, funded at $51 million in FY 98, "conduct applied research and development, provide technical assistance, develop multimedia education materials and other products, and disseminate information in an effort to help others use knowledge from research and practice to improve education."

Although they do not provide direct funding to public and private schools, according to their official program description "the activities undertaken by the centers benefit those schools." Recent data collected by the Department of Education indicate, however, show that the CRACs and the Labs are less than helpful in providing assistance with important issues many states and districts are currently facing, such as standards-based reform, new legislation, and flexibility and accountability provisions in federal legislation (Table 4).

---

[55] Grossen, p. 26.

Table 4

Percent of States and School Districts Who Reported Federally Supported Technical Assistance Centers and Labs to be Either "Not At All Helpful" or Only "A Little Helpful"[56]		CRACs	LABS
Districts	Standards-based Reform	58%	48%
	New Federal Provisions	59%	58%
States	Standards-based Reform	59%	46%
	Flexibility/Accountability	55%	48%

Recent Inspector General Audits of the Education Laboratories have found evidence that their use of federal funds is not always in the best interest of children and supporting what works. A 1998 audit report of the WestEd Regional Laboratory in California found that it did not comply with certain Federal laws and regulations in how it spent federal dollars, and improperly billed the U.S. Government for subcontractor work.[57] WestEd was also found to have improperly spent

- $5,179 to lease a Jeep Grand Cherokee for the Lab's Director
- More than $1,000 on foreign travel and airfare upgrades
- $450 to pay for a Disc Jockey to provide entertainment at the board's two-day staff meeting at a resort

In February 1998 the Inspector General also reported that the University of North Carolina at Greensboro could not justify $2.3 million in federal dollars used for salaries and fringe benefits. It could not provide evidence that an appropriate amount of time and effort was spent to operate the Southeastern Regional Vision for Education (Lab) to justify such costs.[58]

WHAT WORKS: OUTSIDE OF THE BELTWAY

Because of the apparent vacuum of reliable evidence that federal programs are effectively spending tax dollars to improve education, the Subcommittee traveled around the county to hear the perspective of parents, students, teachers, community leaders and administrators on what works and what's wasted. We visited 26 education institutions and heard from more than 225 witnesses in an attempt to gain a better understanding of what parents, teachers and local educators believe is working in America's education system. Witnesses shared many different success stories, but sounded four common themes at every hearing - the keys to educational success:

---

[56] Jane Hannaway with Kristi Kimball, *Reports on Reform from the Field: District and State Survey Results*, Prepared for U.S. Department of Education, Planning and Evaluation Service by The Urban Institute, 1997.
[57] Office of Inspector General, U.S. Department of Education, "WestEd's Administration of the Regional Educational Laboratory Contract," ACN: 09-60009, March 1998.
[58] Office of Inspector General, U.S. Department of Education, "Review of Costs Incurred by the University of North Carolina, Greensboro, and the Southeastern Regional Vision for Education Under the U.S. Department of Education's Regional Laboratories Contract," ACN: 04-70015, February 1998.

- Parental Involvement and Empowerment;
- Local Control;
- Basic academics;
- Dollars to the classroom, not to bureaucracies.

The following section describes how each of these elements contributes to success at the local level.

THE CROSSROADS PROJECT: FINDING SUCCESS AT THE LOCAL LEVEL

Location of Field Hearings
Figure 10

	Crossroads Field Hearing/ Site Visits	Date	Educational Institutions Visited	Witnesses
1	Chicago, Illinois	May 19, 1995	1	13
2	Milwaukee, Wisconsin	October 23, 1995	2	8
3	Napa, California	January 29, 1997	2	11
4	San Fernando, California	January 30, 1997	1	11
5	Phoenix, Arizona	January 37, 1997	2	12
6	Wilmington, Delaware	March 3, 1997	3	14
7	Milledgeville, Georgia	April 22, 1997	2	13
8	Bronx, New York	May 5, 1997	1	15
9	Cincinnati, Ohio	May 27, 1997	3	12
10	Louisville, Kentucky	May 28, 1997	2	11
11	Little Rock, Arkansas	May 29, 1997	2	11
12	Cleveland, Ohio	September 12, 1997	1	30
13	Muskegon Heights, Michigan	October 2, 1997	1	13
14	Des Moines, Iowa	November 3, 1997	1	14
15	Ft. Collins, Colorado	March 20, 1998	2	12
16	Lewisberry, Pennsylvania	March 30, 1998	1	9
	Total for Field Hearings		26	205
	D. C. Crossroads Hearings			
1	Kick-Off Hearing with Lamar Alexander	March 6, 1997	0	2
2	D.C. Schools Hearing	May 1, 1997	0	9
3	Dollars to the Classroom	May 8, 1997	0	7
4	Drugs/Violence Prevention Programs Hearing	June 24, 1997	0	4
5	Teacher Training	July 8, 1997	0	5
6	Literacy (Full Committee)	July 31, 1997	0	5
	Total		26	237

PARENTS INVOLVED IN THEIR CHILDREN'S EDUCATION

> *I think there is an arrogance on the part of the school bureaucracy that assumes that they know best what is for everybody's children. I assume the opposite. I don't think anybody can make a better decision for their children than the parent.*
> -- Mr. Stahl, parent, Napa, California

Research has found that a student whose parent or guardian is involved in their education is more likely to succeed. Parents who take responsibility for ensuring that their children receive a high-quality education are the keys to success at the local level.

- Children in single-parent families are more likely to experience early school problems than children in two-parent families.[59]

- In 1995, 3 - to 5-year-olds living with two biological or adoptive parents were more likely to have been read to three or more times a week, to have been told a story once a week, or to have visited the library in the previous month than 3- to 5-year-olds living with one biological or adoptive parent.[60]

- First- and second-graders aged 6–8 living with one biological or adoptive parent were *more* likely to experience academic problems and to have their parents report that they were academically below the middle of their class than those students living with two biological or adoptive parents.[61]

- Twenty-two percent of children living with divorced mothers must repeat a grade and 30 percent of children born to a single parent must repeat a grade. Only 12 percent of children from two-parent families have to repeat a grade in school.[62]

Unfortunately, the proportion of children raised in two-parent families is declining rapidly. The proportion of children living in single-parent families has more than doubled since 1970. In 1994, 25 percent of children under age 18 lived in single-parent families, while 11 percent did so in 1970. In 1994, 60 percent of black children lived in single parent families compared to 19 percent of white children and 29 percent of Hispanic children.

---

[59] U.S. Department of Education, National Center for Education Statistics, *The Condition of Education 1997* (NCES 97-388), Washington, D.C.: 1997, p. 205, based on NCES, *National Household Education Survey* (NHES), 1995 (Early Childhood Program Participation File).
[60] *Ibid*, p. 208.
[61] *Ibid*, p. 209.
[62] Debra Dawson, "Family Structure and Children's Well-Being: Data from the 1988 National Health Interview Survey," *Journal of Marriage and Family,* Vol. 53, 1991.

What this means is that children from all backgrounds are facing increasingly difficult family situations, making it more difficult to learn, and all the more important that schools are as effective as possible. The data show that even children from two-parent, low-income families out-perform students from high income families headed by a single parent.[63] As family cohesiveness declines, so will academic performance.

When a parent is involved in their child's educational experience, it only strengthens their academic progress. Federal programs that attempt to provide a substitute for parents actually may have the negative effect of distancing parents from a child's educational experience, from school breakfasts to after-school care.

Catholic Schools: A Model of Parental Involvement

At a national average of $2,178 a year, tuition at Catholic schools is lower than all other forms of private education. Yet these schools have been teaching children with successful results regardless of their background. Because costs are kept as low as possible, schools must rely on parents to provide many of the "extras" that parents have come to take for granted in public education. Relying on parents, however, is not considered by Catholic school principals to be a liability. Rather, they see it as one of the reasons for their success in the midst of adverse economic and social conditions.

At the Kentucky hearing, Sister Amelia Stenger described the role of parental involvement in the success of Catholic schools.

> *Catholic schools depend on the involvement and resources of parents more than they depend on any government agency. Parents advise the principal and the pastor on policies of the school, they volunteer their time to extracurricular activities for the students and they greatly assist faculty and staff. Many of the activities in which parents are involved could not take place without their assistance. Often schools cannot afford to pay someone to take care of these activities, therefore our parents are our most vital resource.*

Dependence on parental involvement for day-to-day educational activities provides a built-in accountability mechanism for the schools - they cannot operate without the parents and therefore cannot ignore their presence.

Removing Barriers to Parental Involvement

Successful schools with high levels of parental involvement find that removing barriers to involvement is an important factor of their success. English instruction, literacy classes, student-

---

[63] *One Parent Families and Their Children: The School's Most Significant Minority,* The Consortium for the Study of School Needs of Children from One-Parent Families, Arlington, VA, 1980.

parent classes, and job training are a few of the ways in which schools have involved parents who were previously on the periphery of school activities. Mr. Joe Lucente, the principal of a charter school in the heart of Los Angeles, described how his school attempted to include as many parents as possible:

> *Before we became a charter school, yes, that [only certain parents volunteering] was a problem. However, when we became a charter school, we opened up a variety of vehicles for parental involvement...If your need was to learn English, we had English classes. If your need was basic literacy, we had literacy classes.*

Ms. Earl Lene Jones, a fifth-grade public school teacher in Napa, California, testified that parental support was "critical in all aspects of educating the child." She described a hands-on parental involvement program in her school:

> *At our school we have something called the* Child and Parents Succeeding Program*...the parent or guardian or caretaker comes in and sits right next to the child during the course of a school day. They sit with the child and help the child stay focused, help the child to read, help the child to work problems. We found this is quite effective, but lets the other children see that there is involvement and caring from parents.*

Mrs. Beverly Tunney, a Chicago public school principal observed that making parents comfortable - especially low-income parents - is very important:

> *As the parents have become more comfortable in the school setting and experience the excitement of learning, we have found a higher rate of parents volunteering within Healy [School] and a base group of parents that have an expanded knowledge of curriculum, the learning process, and raising children.*[64]

Mrs. Cleaster Mims, principal of the Marva Collins Preparatory School in Cincinnati testified that her school *expected* participation by the parents: "We...believe that parents should be actively involved, so our organization or our school expects parent participation. We do not see parents as intruders...we strongly believe that parents should know each day what is happening with their children when they entrust them to us."

Encouraging Parental Involvement in Phoenix

ATOP Academy is a public charter school in Phoenix that serves a mostly African-American population in the inner city. The school has been very successful and currently has a waiting list

---

[64] Subcommittee on Oversight and Investigations, Committee on Education and the Workforce, *Hearing on Leading Edge Practices in Education*, U.S. House of Representatives, 104th Congress, No. 104-38, Chicago, IL, May 19, 1995, p. 30.

of some 175 students. When students come to the school, parents are asked to agree to the following as part of their involvement in the school:[65]

1. Restrict television watching during the week.
2. Spend 15-20 minutes on school nights reading to their children.
3. Attend all parent-teacher conferences.
4. Attend Parent Involvement Committee monthly meetings.
5. Participate in their child's classroom activities.

This up-front commitment encourages parents to be involved, giving them very specific tasks to accomplish and build upon.

School Choice: Parental Choices In Control

> *Can anyone name one public school in Ohio that has closed because of poor performance?*
> *-- Kenneth Blackwell, Treasurer of State of Ohio*

The Subcommittee visited the two cities where publicly funded school-choice programs have been implemented, Milwaukee and Cleveland, as examples of parental choice bringing about true local control.

While it is still too early to determine the full extent of the impact school choice will have on the children in these cities, initial studies have found that children attending the school of their choice have measurably improved academic achievement.

Both sides of the school choice debate recognize that when parents select the school their child attends, they are more satisfied (Table 5). Nationally, the U.S. Department of Education found this to be the case by wide margins:

Table 5

Percentage of parents of students in grades 3-12 who were very satisfied with aspects of their child's school: 1993[66]	
Chosen Public School	61.2
Chosen Private School	82.5
Assigned Public School	52.3

Choice, particularly in many center cities, provides what is perhaps the only remaining avenue to a good education: private schools. True equity and access in education is achieved when parents are allowed to make choices about their children's education. To define "access"

---

[65] Testimony of Raymond Jackson, PhD. *Education at a Crossroads: What Works and What's Wasted*, Subcommittee on Oversight and Investigations, Committee on Education and the Workforce, U.S. House of Representatives, 105th Congress, No. 105-11, January 31, 1997, p. 471.
[66] National Center of Education Statistics, *The Condition of Education 1996*, Table 4-4.

and "equity" exclusively in terms of public schools is to miss out on the overall objective of education: children learning.

Paving the Way in Milwaukee

In April 1990, Wisconsin Gov. Tommy Thompson signed legislation which enacted the Milwaukee Parental Choice Program. This program provides state funding for low-income children in the city to attend private, nonsectarian schools of choice. Spearheaded by Rep. Annette "Polly" Williams, a Democrat from Milwaukee, the program has survived several rounds of Constitutional challenges and has expanded every year since its inception. The American Civil Liberties Union (ACLU), National Association for the Advancement of Colored People (NAACP) and the National Education Association (NEA) filed a suit which until recently prevented the program from expanding from 1,650 to 15,000 students, as signed into law by Gov. Thompson in 1995.

In response to the court injunction, which prevented the program from expanding, in order to accommodate the overwhelming demand, people in Wisconsin donated more than $1.6 million to Partners Advancing Values in Education (PAVE). This private organization gave 50 percent scholarships to about 2,000 low-income students who had enrolled in religious schools under the expanded voucher program. Still, this amount was not nearly enough to accommodate the demand of those parents who wanted to start sending their children to private schools, but who were still in the public school system.

On June 10, 1998, the Wisconsin Supreme Court ruled that students could use state-funded scholarships to attend religious schools of their choice, clearing the way for expansion of the program to 15,000 students. The court affirmed the primacy of parental choice in directing where the vouchers are spent. Judge Donald Seinmetz wrote for the court that "not one cent flows from the state to a sectarian private school...except as a result of the necessary and intervening choices of individual parents."[67]

In 1995, the Committee held a hearing on school choice to provide low-income families the same opportunities that those who can afford a private school education currently enjoy. School choice empowers parents, and allows them to make the decisions concerning the education of their children. Ms. Pilar Gonzalez, a Milwaukee parent, described the need for local control and parental empowerment:

> *[Milwaukee Public Schools have] become an educational prison for many low-income families while providing our children with only a mediocre curriculum. This must change and we as parents must assume the responsibility for that together.*

---

[67] Jaon Biskupic, "Wisconsin Court Widens School Vouchers' Scope," *The Washington Post*, June 11, 1998, p. A1.

Ms. Zakiya Courtney, the director of Parents for Choice added that:

We need more options for our children. Not fewer. We believe the role of the federal government in education is to respect parents and support their choice in education for their children.

In February 1996, data from the Milwaukee school choice experiment were made available to the public. Professors Jay P. Greene of the University of Houston Center for Public Policy and Paul E. Peterson of Harvard University's Program in Education Policy and Governance conducted a detailed assessment of this information. Their study found:

- Reading scores of choice students who had participated in the program three and four years, on average, scored 3 to 5 percentile points higher, respectively, than those of comparable low-income public school students;

- Math scores, on average, were 5 and 12 percentile points higher, respectively.

The implications of these findings are extremely significant. As Greene and Peterson note, "If similar success could be achieved for all minority students nationwide, it could close the gap separating white and minority test scores by somewhere between one-third and more than one-half."[68]

Finding Hope in Cleveland

After spending billions of dollars and producing decades of failure, the Cleveland Public School System is perhaps one of the best examples of what is not working in education. Since 1978, $1.1 billion in state and local tax dollars has been spent on its desegregation program, one of the most expensive in the nation. In a system where 80 percent of the students are in poverty, and 20 percent change addresses each year, only one in three Cleveland students receives a high school diploma. On any given day, nearly one in six students are absent. Twelve percent of the city's ninth-graders passed all required state proficiency tests in 1995, compared to 54 percent for the entire state. Of Cleveland's eighth-graders in 1990-91, 46 percent had dropped out by 1995, and only 7 percent graduated and passed the 12th grade proficiency test.

To address the failures of this dying school system, Ohio Gov. George Voinovich signed a two-year budget package in 1995 that created a $5 million pilot voucher program. This particular voucher program was the first in the nation to include religious schools. Low-income students can receive up to 90 percent of private-school tuition cost, and all other Cleveland students are eligible to receive vouchers worth 75 percent of tuition.

Nearly two years after the 1995 hearing in Milwaukee, 21 parents, students, teachers, administrators, state and local officials lined up to testify on behalf of the successes of the state-

---

[68] Jay P. Greene and Paul E. Peterson, "The Effectiveness of School Choice in Milwaukee: A Secondary Analysis of Data from the Program's Evaluation," American Political Science Association Panel on the Political Analysis of Urban School Systems, August-September 1996.

funded Cleveland Scholarship and Tutoring Program. Included for the record were more than 50 letters, primarily from recipients of scholarships, testifying to how their education has changed for the better under the voucher system.

Many witnesses shared experiences similar to Adasha Bias, third-grade student at Hope Central Academy. She told of how she was unable to learn in her public school because children were always disrupting class. And even though they had computers at her old school, at Hope they did not just have games—technology provided learning tools used to instruct them in math and reading.

Testimony of Adasha Bias

Hello. My name is Adasha Bias. I am in third grade. This is my second year at Hope Central Academy. I've learned a lot at Hope.

In my old school, the kids were bad! They threw things, got into fights all the time, and we didn't get to learn. I feel safe here!

There is no fighting, and the kids don't throw things. At my old school, we had computers, but they only had games. At Hope, our computers have math, reading and language. I really love our computers.

I love my teachers because they work really hard with us. We do projects here. I never did projects in my old school.

So far my grades have been outstanding. My favorite subjects are reading and math. Please help us keep up the good work, and keep our school open. Thank you.

Ms. Ballard-Hunt, a single mother of four children, shared how her children's behavior and learning improved when they were able to attend Hope Academy through Cleveland Scholarship Tutoring Program. Diagnosed as having behavior problems and in need of counseling while in public school, her daughter Antonice had no interest in school and was a D and F student. At Hope her behavior problems were brought under control through the concerted efforts of her teacher and principal. She can now read better than her mother. Her first-grader who did not know the alphabet learned to read within a few months. Ms. Ballard-Hunt told the Subcommittee that the scholarship program "opens up opportunities for the future of our children...it has helped keep my daughters alive."[69]

Ms. Bert Holt, director of the Cleveland Scholarship and Tutoring Program, described a system where parents were finally able to be in charge of their children's education. "The Scholarship Voucher Choice Program is indeed evolving and producing revolutionary results. The parents are happy. They are in charge...Parents are taking responsibility for themselves and their children. They are making choices and accepting consequences."

Delvoland Shakespeare, a parent of children attending a Cleveland Catholic school and recently profiled by *The Wall Street Journal*, gave a heartfelt account of his sacrifices to send his children to a "working" school:

> *When I look on the news...I see a mayor who is trying to take over our school system and now lawsuits are being raised up. We don't have time for that...each and every day...my child misses out on a day of education that he should have. I took it upon myself before the voucher program even existed to take the little resources that me and my wife has to send our child to a private school. It was hard for me...That was my choice...it was worth it...I want my child to have the best opportunity he possibly can.*[70]

Councilwoman Fanny Lewis, the leader of the fight to bring choice to Cleveland also testified:

> *I am convinced that nobody can educate us but us. If we are not involved in the educational process of our youngsters, they are not going to be educated properly.*

Chosen at random to receive the scholarships, low-income children attending Hope Academy experienced significant gains in reading and math, according to a Harvard University study released in June 1997. Students in kindergarten through third grade after one year scored, on average, 5.5 percentile points higher on standardized reading tests and 15 percentile points higher in math. All children in all grades improved. This is a stark contrast to other studies that have

---

[69] Testimony of Ms. Ballard, *Field Hearing on "Education At A Crossroads,"* Cleveland, Ohio, September 12, 1997, No. 105-57, p. 30.

[70] Testimony of Devloland Shakespeare, *Field Hearing...*, Cleveland, Ohio, September 12, 1997, No. 105-57, p. 32. See also: Amity Shales, "A Change to Equip My Child," *The Wall Street Journal*, February 23, 1998, p. A22.

shown that students with comparable backgrounds tend to lose an average of one to two percentile points each year that they are in school.[71]

Parents Teaching Their Children at Home

Many parents are involved in their children's education at home: Home schooling is one of the fastest growing educational movements in the United States. A study conducted in 1996 Home School Legal Defense Association estimated the number of home schooling students at 1.23 million. Because of growth trends it is now estimated that there are 1.5 million home schooled-children in the United States. The study points out that "there are more home school students nationwide that there are public school students in Wyoming, Vermont, Delaware, North Dakota, Alaska, South Dakota, Rhode Island, Montana, and Hawaii - combined."[72]

Not only is home schooling spreading to diverse segments of society, they have performed well on standardized tests. Of the 1997 graduating class, the American College Test High School Profile Report found that home-educated students averaged 22.5 on the ACT while the national average is 21. A perfect score is a 36.

The Federal Role

The testimony of witnesses demonstrates that the best models of parental involvement are locally driven. More often than not the principal of the school, who knows the parents, primarily drives the level of parental involvement. No witnesses asked for federal dollars to increase parental involvement. It is clear that programs from Washington are unable to emulate parental involvement, no matter how hard these programs try.

School choice is another very important component of empowering parents. It allows parents to decide where their children should attend the school where they believe their child will receive the best education possible. The school choice programs examined by the Subcommittee, as well as others, were brought into being by local parents - without federal dollars or encouragement.

Local, state, and federal governments must ensure that their programs and policies do not make it harder for parents to fulfill their responsibilities to their children. It must ensure that it is not burdening principals and teachers, impeding them from making his or her school as child-centered as possible. Parents who wish to teach their children at home should be free to do so without burdensome requirements and unnecessary government oversight. Parents who wish to send their children to safe, drug-free and effective schools should be allowed to make that choice. Providing as many opportunities as possible for parents to be a part of their child's education will help increase accountability, and will help more children to receive a high-quality education.

---

[71] Jay P. Greene, Paul E. Petersen, and William Howell, "An Evaluation of the Cleveland Scholarship Program," Harvard University Program in Education Policy and Governance, September 1997.
[72] Dr. Brian Ray, *Home Education Across the United States*, (Washington, D.C.: Home School Legal Defense Association), 1997.

As former Secretaries of Education William Bennett and Lamar Alexander told the Committee on Economic and Educational Opportunities in 1995:

> *[E]xcept when the civil rights of individuals are menaced, the federal government should never impede the capacity of families, teachers, communities and states to decide how best to provide education to their children, and should never substitute its judgment for theirs.*[73]

---

[73] Lamar Alexander and William J. Bennett, *Hearing on Reexamining Old Assumptions*, Committee on Education and the Workforce, Subcommittee on Oversight and Investigations, No. 104-7, p. 14.

LOCAL CONTROL, LOCAL ACCOUNTABILITY

> *The handcuffs have been taken off, yes, but we are in a fishbowl too. Everyone watches what we do and how we do it, and we do it very well, and we do it very well because we have local control. We set the policy at the local level, and we have control over where the money goes and how it is spent.*
> -- Mr. Joe Lucente, LA Charter School Principal
>
> **Mr. McKeon: The superintendent doesn't have any say over you? Who is your boss?**
> **Mr. Lucente: 160 staff members, the community, *1300 parents...***

Parents who are involved in their children's education know what is working and what is not. Monitoring their child's progress by spending time in their classroom and observing school operations gives the parent a good opportunity to see how effectively their child is being educated. A high level of accountability is therefore in place when parents are involved, which facilitates local control and oversight.

Charter Schools: Autonomy In Exchange For Accountability

> *It is a waiver of all waivers...this autonomy is in exchange for accountability.*
> -- Dr. Yvonne Chan, Principal, Los Angeles Unified School District

At the hearing in Los Angeles, Calif., which primarily focused on Charter Schools, the Subcommittee heard about what has taken place in the relatively new movement of charter schools. Mr. Premack, Director of the Charter Schools Project, Institute for Education Reform, was responsible for conducting a review of the charter schools in the state of California. He argued that while charter schools are not a panacea, they have cut back on bureaucracy and provide a new level of accountability not often found in public schools:

> *We have taken a 6,000-page, 13-volume Education Code and a variety of other codes and launched all of them...[I]n exchange for that comes accountability...the school is accountable for results. They operate under a limited term, usually a five-year contract called a charter; and if the students don't learn, the charter is not renewed or revoked - a pretty powerful concept...the schools put a lot on the line, [teachers] are putting their jobs on the line for student performance. In exchange, the handcuffs are gone, the*

> *regulations are gone…charter schools are public schools that operate under public operating principles.*

Removing bureaucracy facilitates local innovation and the implementation of local solutions to local problems. As Ms. Sharon Ramano, a teacher at the Wildcat Academy in New York described it,

> *We're structured differently…you don't have to call up every time and wait six weeks for an idea to go through. You basically do what you have to do and you have the whole autonomy to be able to…you have paperwork and you are held accountable, but I just don't think we are held hostage, time-wise, scheduling-wise, we're not held hostage.*

Good Intentions Do Not Always Lead To Good Results

Good intentions without accountability do not necessarily lead to success. Mr. Flanigan is the Chairman of the School Choice Foundation Inc, in New York. He described how he and his wife adopted a sixth-grade class in the "I Have a Dream" national program. They guaranteed to send any child from their adopted class, who graduated from high school, to college free of charge. Of the 48 kids in this class, only one completed college. Mr. Flanigan characterized the program as a failure.

This experience led Mr. Flanigan to seek a program that did work. What he found was that the inner-city Catholic school system had remarkable success with underprivileged kids. Because of this, Mr. Flanigan decided to start a scholarship program, Student-Sponsor Partnerships, which provide high school scholarships to inner-city children from impoverished and primarily single parent families. The program has thus far graduated 1,000 scholarship recipients, and 75 percent have gone to four-year colleges. Mr. Flanigan credited this kind of success with the fact that the Catholic schools are about "freedom." Students and teachers choose to be where they are; principals choose which teachers to employ. Based on his experience, he testified that:

> *When schools are accountable, the parents and students who have the freedom to choose where they wish to be educated, they will become good schools. If schools do not meet the requirements of those parents and their students, they will and should close.*[74]

An audit of Mr. Flanigan's scholarship program by the RAND Corporation found that the scholarship recipients were of the same demographic background as those who attended zoned public schools in inner-city New York. After four years in the public schools, only the top 10 percent of the senior class took the SAT, scoring an average combined score of 642 out of 1600. Scholarship recipients who moved a few blocks away to private schools scored an average of 803, and 60 percent of those students took the test.

---

[74] Testimony of Peter Flanigan, *Education at a Crossroads*, Bronx, New York, May 5, 1997, No. 105-32.

Investing in the Future: Community Involvement in Arkansas

Business and community partnerships with schools and students in their community are also examples of "what works" about local control. Community involvement can come in many different forms: funding, volunteers, apprenticeship opportunities, as well as community pride, which encourages students to succeed.

Many witnesses at the Arkansas hearing spoke of the importance of community collaboration with schools. One program called STRIVE operates in conjunction with the University of Arkansas at Little Rock. The goal of this program is to give teachers a better idea of what the business community wants and needs by actually bringing the teachers to the businesses. As a result they have seen students gain in math and science.

Dr. Charles Adair, a school superintendent testified that community ownership is crucial:

> *[P]ublic schools are for all parties involved to feel a partnership, whether it be administrators, teachers, parents, businesses, patrons, grandparents, students or school board members. The school belongs to all residents of the school district and for it to work all should feel ownership.* [75]

A local school board member surmised, "[I]f the initiative for improving the schools were shifted to these communities, I believe the people would respond in an even greater fashion."

The Federal Role

Georgia's Secretary of Education, Dr. Linda Schrenko, perhaps summed up local control the best when she told the Subcommittee while in rural Milledgeville, GA:

> *[T]he most frequent message I have heard is that no one can make better decisions about local education than the parents, teachers, and students in those local communities... It is my heartfelt belief that locally controlled programs have and always will do a better job of meeting local education needs... I call for our federal governments to recognize that local decisions yield some of the highest quality education results.* [76]

Parents involved in their children's education, either as volunteers, choosing their child's school, helping with their homework, or teaching them at home, will have a close view of whether their children are receiving a good education. Local school officials who know they are being held in close scrutiny will make decisions based on local needs. The federal government is

---

[75] Testimony of Dr. Charles Adair, *Field Hearing on Education at a Crossroads*, Committee on Education and the Workforce, Little Rock, AR, May 29, 1997, No. 105-34.
[76] Testimony of Superintendent Linda Schrenko, *Field Hearing on Education at a Crossroads*, Committee on Education and the Workforce, Milledgeville, GA, April 22, 1997, No. 105-16.

further away from students and local accountability and as a result has created "one-size fits all" programs and policies, which fail to give local educators the flexibility to adapt to unique local needs. Accountability must be "created" through regulations and requirements, which leads to the bureaucracy and paperwork schools are faced with today, diverting the focus from accountability and results to process and compliance. Schools and school districts that have designed innovative solutions to effectively address their unique problems have often done so in spite of such bureaucratic oversight, not because of it.

MASTERING THE BASICS

Throughout the hearings the Subcommittee found another characteristic of successful schools to be a focus on "mastering the basics"—making sure students can read well and do basic math at early grades and then go on to do more complex work. When education becomes less child-centered and more controlled by administrators and bureaucrats, more interests dictate what children should be learning such that by the end of the day they have spent only a fraction of their time in school on basic academics.

Successful schools have implemented research-based academic programs that improve children's academic performance, and have stayed away from faddish programs that produce inadequate results.

The Importance of Effective Reading Instruction

The Subcommittee heard from several witnesses who described at the California hearings the detrimental effects of instructing children to read using "whole language" methods of instruction. In the 1980s, California used a teaching method called "whole language," almost to the complete exclusion of phonics instruction. "Phonics" refers to teaching methods that instruct beginning readers how to break unfamiliar words into letters and sounds. "Whole language" teaching methods in their most basic form teach a child to read by learning words in the context of literature. Recent research findings by Dr. Reid Lyon of the National Institute for Child Health and Human Development, as well as many others, have shown that effective reading instruction must include phonics.

After having just implemented whole-language based reading instruction in the 1980s, California recently switched back to phonics-based instruction. In 1996, it allocated $52 million for textbooks and teacher training to make the switch. Such a dramatic turn around is understandable: after having been near the top for years, California reading scores plummeted to a ranking of 49 out of the 50 states. Both Democrats and Republicans argue that this focus on whole language and lack of emphasis on phonics is one of the primary reasons for California's poor test scores in reading. Indeed, many states that have used whole language in the past are facing the same problem of low reading test scores: in the last two years, 67 bills have been proposed in state houses around the country that would require phonics to be a component of reading instruction.[77]

In Los Angeles, the Subcommittee heard from a parent who described how her children who learned to read after whole language instruction was implemented, failed to excel despite her best efforts:

---

[77] Kathleen Manzo, "More States Moving to Make Phonics the Law," *Education Week*, April 29, 1998.

> *As a front-line parent with six children in public school from first grade to the University...Some of my kids are highly motivated, some only minimally motivated – and that with parental pressure. They've grown up in a literature-rich environment, with minimal TV watching. I have read to them almost daily. I earned a teaching credential myself...I have been on School Site Councils, PTA boards, and a classroom volunteer. Still, I could not prevent my children from suffering some of the effects of a lousy curriculum and a poor pedagogy.[78]*

Children need to have a firm grasp of the basic tools that enable them to move on to advanced subjects. Those who fail to master these skills, especially those from impoverished backgrounds, will only fall further behind. Mr. Joseph Schulze, Superintendent of Muskegon Public Schools in Michigan, testified that children must learn the basics before moving on to other issues:

> *[Their priority] first and foremost is to educate students to read with understanding, to write with clarity, to compute with accuracy, to communicate effectively and understand our history and culture and to live responsibly in this civility. These objectives must be met first before we assume other challenges.*

Knowing how to read is the most basic component of learning, and children who advance from grade to grade without knowing how to read are being robbed of the most essential skill they need to succeed in life. Knowing what works in reading instruction is therefore critical. California is an example of a state that was finally willing to acknowledge what was not working, replacing whole language with research-based phonics instruction, putting children first and rather than a particular philosophy of teaching.

Core Knowledge: Equity in Knowledge, Equity in Education

In Pennsylvania and Colorado, the Subcommittee heard from parents whose children attend school schools that have implemented the "Core Knowledge Sequence" program, a curriculum that is the result of research into the highest performing elementary school systems around the world. Several parents described how their children advanced in knowledge at a faster pace and in a more systematic manner than their other children who were not a part of the program.

The Core Knowledge Sequence is based on the principle that true equity in education can be achieved only when children are taught a "common" curriculum— a curriculum that builds on knowledge at each grade level to develop a consistency of learning seldom seen in traditional elementary school curricula. There are presently more than 700 schools in 43 states that have implemented Core Knowledge as their curriculum. An estimated 80 percent of those schools are public.

---

[78] Testimony of Gayle Cloud, *Education at a Crossroads,* Riverside, California, January 30, 1997, p. 242.

According to the Core Knowledge Foundation, it seeks to "provide children, regardless of background, with the shared knowledge they need to be included in our national literate culture."[79] Many children from impoverished backgrounds enter school at a severe disadvantage to other children because they are not familiar with the broad body of knowledge that most speakers and writers take for granted that people understand. Ensuring that all children have access to this knowledge prevents them from falling farther behind their more advantaged peers. In addition, the specific skills and knowledge children learn in each grade allow teachers and parents to determine the progress of their children.

Charter Schools: Free to Focus on the Basics

Because of their relative autonomy, many charter schools around the country are able to focus basic academics in ways their public school counterparts are not.

In fact, many charters have made such a focus one of their primary selling points.

Dr. Raymond Jackson, the CEO of the ATOP Academy Charter School in Phoenix, AZ, described how, after 25 years in public education, he started a public charter school which now has 300 students and an additional 175 on a waiting list.

ATOP is one of the most successful charter schools, emphasizing basic academics, a strict discipline code, small classroom size, and heavy parental involvement. It serves a largely minority student population. Both certified and non-certified teachers are used and the students dress in uniforms each day. Mr. Jackson explained that they were able to teach their kindergartners to read because they take time to diagnose their level of reading as well as the degree to which they may be frustrated.

At the ATOP Academy, they do not just "talk" about learning—they see it happening every day. Their focus is on results, not process or matching their programs to federal guidelines and priorities. Mr. Jackson described for the Committee how his school is different in this way:

> *In most schools, the language of the classroom is primarily a language about the process of teaching something. It is not itself a language of learning. We came to call this language 'talkinabout' because we saw so many people talking about reading, but not actually reading, talking about writing, but not actually writing. Talkinabout is an abstract language...it is a rumor about learning...We talk about people learning, but we are not actually teaching kids how to learn.*

---

[79] See: *www.coreknowldege.org*

The Importance of Literature: Marva Collins Prep in Cincinnati, Ohio

Opened in the basement of a Baptist church in 1990 with 44 students, the non-sectarian Marva Collins Prep School in Cincinnati has been described by many as a "miracle school." Children at this school are primarily from disadvantaged backgrounds and are 99 percent minority, yet they score two to six grade levels above their entrance level scores. But according to Mrs. Mims, the school's CEO, it should not be seen as a "miracle" when:

- Three- and four-year olds know their multiplication tables;
- Kindergartners read *The Secret Garden;*
- Third- and fourth-graders read and understand Homer's *Odyssey.*

Ms. Mims described for the Subcommittee how parents would bring their children to her school who were diagnosed as having "Attention Deficit Disorder" in order to avoid having to give them medication. At Marva Collins, these students have become avid readers and critical thinkers.

Mrs. Mims credits their success largely to the importance they place on studying the great works of literature. From a young age, children are reading Shakespeare and learning to appreciate great books. *See Spot Run* type books have been replaced entirely by the classics. Money, while important, was not the essential component assuring their success.

Houston: Basic Academics and Phonics Raise Test Scores

In the Acres Homes section of Houston is a shining example of what works in education. With a proven track record for more than two decades, Wesley Elementary serves children in a violent and drug-infested neighborhood in Houston. The school is 99 percent minority and 90 percent of its students qualify for free or reduced school lunches. Despite these circumstances which usually predict low achievement levels, Wesley test scores are consistently among the highest in the state. In 1996, 100 percent of Wesley's students passed the Texas Assessment of Academic Skills (TAAS) in reading, easily surpassing the statewide passing rate of 70 percent for schools with similar demographics. It is not uncommon to find kindergartners reading 2nd grade books. Although 10 percent of Houston students are found to need special education, only three percent of Wesley students are in special education classes. These results are achieved at a cost of $2,500 per child, which is $1,000 less than the district average.[80]

Mr. Thaddeus Lott became the principal of Wesley in 1975, when only 18 percent of its third-graders were at or above grade level in reading. Deciding that "it's a myth that if you're born community and your skin is a certain color that you can't achieve on a higher level," he aggressively implemented the proven method of instruction known as "direct instruction" or DISTAR.[81] His formula for success centered on basic academics, and includes rigorous teacher training, strict discipline, and high expectations. In a typical classroom, "the pace is quick, the goals are set high, and no disruptions are tolerated." By 1980, test scores in both reading and

---

[80] Tyce Palmaffy, "No Excuses," *Policy Review*, January 1998.
[81] *Ibid.*

vocabulary were above the 80th percentile - more than 40 points higher than the scores of similar schools. Today, due to its continued success, parents desperate to give their children an opportunity to excel often resort to lying about where they live in order to get their children in Wesley.[82]

Mr. Lott has been consistently successful because he has not been swayed by the rise and fall of various education fads and progressive education methods which view learning as a child-centered "discovery" process, de-emphasizing correct answers and "basic" skills.[83] He divides his students in classes by ability, ensuring that teachers do not need to develop lesson plans for more than three skill levels. New teachers receive rigorous training and are held accountable, as Mr. Lott places a high priority on tracking progress and tests students on a regular basis.

Despite Wesley's proven record using DISTAR, the school had to hold candy sales and delay technology purchases to purchase curriculum materials because it was not a "state-approved" curricula. Now, however, Wesley is a charter school and Mr. Lott has the flexibility to spend its curriculum dollars on the curriculum that works.

The Houston School District recently implemented a uniform strategy for reading instruction in all schools and grades that emphasizes basic skills. Reading in grades K-3 must be taught in an uninterrupted block of at least 90 minutes each day, with six "prongs" to its approach: phonemic awareness, print, alphabetic and orthographic awareness, comprehension strategies and reading practice. The goal is to have all children reading at grade level by the third grade.[84]

Early results of the new reading curriculum have been encouraging. In spite of the daunting obstacles that are often present in a district where 65 percent of the students qualify for free or reduced price lunches, student test scores have increased steadily at all grade levels, and in some cases dramatically. Fourth-graders have improved 11 percentage points since 1996, the year before the new mandate went into effect, with 89 percent now meeting the minimum standards of the reading test.

The Federal Role: Reliable, Replicable Research Based Practices

When it comes to encouraging basic academics, again there is little the federal government can or ought to do directly at the local level. Instead, it can take steps to ensure that it is not *discouraging* basic academics by not tying federal dollars to "faddish" teaching methods such as whole language. Ensuring that federal dollars are spent to fund research or teacher training that advances research-based teaching methods is one way to accomplish this. When parents are given a voice and the opportunity to hold teachers and schools accountable, they most effectively will ensure that children are being taught the basics.

---

[82] *Ibid.*
[83] The American Federation of Teachers, *Building on the Best, Learning from What Works: Seven Promising Reading and English Language Arts Programs*, January 1998.
[84] Kathleen Kennedy Manzo, "Drilling in Texas," *Education Week*, June 10, 1998.

DOLLARS FOR CLASSROOMS, NOT BUREAUCRATS

> *Don't swamp us with the paperwork and we can have a lot more money going to the kids.*
> *-- Dr. Yvonne Chan, Vaughan Learning Center, California*

Despite the billions of dollars spent on federal education programs over the last two decades, there is still little evidence demonstrating its effect on student achievement. In other words, there is not any evidence that tax dollars were more effectively spent in federal programs than they would have been had the dollars never left the state. Moreover, federal programs force states to comply with many rules and regulations, and often favor larger school districts who can afford to hire "professional" grant writers to win grant awards.

The Subcommittee found that schools have been most successful when they have been able to implement child-centered spending priorities, cutting through bureaucracy and battling cumbersome requirements.

$1.2 Million More for the Children

One of the most successful stories the Subcommittee heard was that of Dr. Yvonne Chan, Principal of the Vaughn Learning Center in Los Angeles, California. The Vaughn Learning Center is located in a community that is a federally-designated "Empowerment Zone" due to its extreme poverty and high crime status and in 1990, was cited as one of the worst schools in the L.A. Unified Schools District. Ninety-five percent of the students are Hispanic.[85]

Dr. Chan described what it was like before her school became a charter school. She testified, "I thought my job was teaching reading, writing, and arithmetic...my real job was the three Bs: Busing, Budget, and But." The "but" came into play when she would say, "I've got an idea about how to improve something," the answer she was given was that's a good idea "but." She told the Subcommittee that as a Charter School, "All that has changed...we are not like before, a black hole of resources."

As a charter school principal, Dr. Chan told her school district, "if you can't give us the dollars then give us the freedom." In their first year they saved $1.2 million by cutting waste and putting children first. With the help of reformed gang members in their community, they installed a computer system of 212 computers all connected to the internet. Parents helped to build 14 classrooms in 10 months, and extended the number of days in class from 163 days to 200.

Nearly all of Dr. Chan's students receive free lunches as part of the federally funded school lunch program. But because five out of 1,200 children did not qualify they had to spend $80,000 to keep track of the five. She asked the question, "How much does it cost to feed five?" She

---

[85] Testimony of Dr. Yyonne Chan, *Field Hearing on Education at a Crossroads*, , Subcommittee on Oversight and Investigations, Committee on Education and the Workforce, January 30, 1997, No. 105-11.

estimated at most, $2,000. They now implement what she calls universal feeding where they feed all of the students and position the $78,000 for some better use.

Dr. Chan concluded her testimony by saying, "we are the poorest school in the district and yet the test scores continue to rise and there is almost perfect attendance."

Changing the way they spent their resources as a school was fundamental to turning Vaughn into a school that focused on children and learning. Eliminating waste and spending dollars on the classroom changed the climate of Vaughn into one of parental involvement and learning.

Tracking Dollars to the Classroom in South Carolina

Dr. Barbara Nielsen, Superintendent of Education for the State of South Carolina, discussed her state's efforts to track dollars to the classroom at the Subcommittee's "Dollars to the Classroom" hearing in Washington, D.C. She outlined many promising initiatives that will improve education in her state, but stated:

> *[P]erhaps the single most important step we have taken toward that goal is to encourage our state to take a hard, clear look at how we spend the money we have, to see if our resources are serving children as efficiently and effectively as possible.*[86]

They accomplished this by adopting an accounting system produces "user-friendly" information about how they spend their education dollars. In 1995 South Carolina became the first state in the nation to implement the In$ite accounting product.[87] The system takes a "mass of data organized for regulatory accounting" and for the first time, "tells us where the money really goes." The system allows them to target their funding better by understanding where the dollars go, ultimately putting children at the center of funding issues rather than requirement.[88]

Table 6

South Carolina Tracks Dollars to the Classroom		
Spending Category	Per Pupil	Percent of Total
Face-to-face teaching	$2,705	49.34%
Classroom materials	$201	3.67%
Pupil Support: Guidance and Counseling	$124	2.27%
Pupil Support: Library, extracurricular, health	$261	6.85%
Teacher Support: Curriculum Development	$104	1.90%
Operations: Non-instructional pupil services	$452	8.25%
Operations: Facilities	$449	8.19%
Leadership (School, program and district management)	$431	7.87%

---

[86] Testimony of Dr. Barbara Nielsen, *Hearing on Dollars to the Classroom*, Subcommittee on Oversight and Investigations, Committee on Education and the Workforce, May 8, 1997, No. 105-27.
[87] In$ite was developed by Coopers & Lybrand, L.L.P.
[88] See http://www.state.sc.us/sde/fam/linkpage.htm for additional details on the In$ite findings in South Carolina.

South Carolina is currently tracking administrative costs at the state level in order to reduce state administrative costs to less than one percent of the budget. South Carolina presently sends 98.5 percent to school districts. The state is encouraging districts to implement this accounting system in order to reduce their costs to less than five percent of their total budgets.

Table 7

South Carolina: State Department of Education Spending	
Spending Category	**Per Pupil**
Teacher Support	$13
Program Support	$19
Data Processing, Business Operations	$10
Program Development	$19
Leadership	$4
District Management	$4

In$ite, perhaps most importantly, provides the public with understandable, valuable information, increasing their ability to participate in the discussion of important education decisions. Information from the system is available to all, and is even posted on the Internet.

The next step in this process is to develop a methodology for a "productivity quotient" for all schools and districts. This system would combine student achievement data with cost data in order to show to taxpayers how much return their investment is producing, in terms of student learning.

South Carolina is now helping hundreds of other school districts and states interested in implementing this system. The system is already in place in several other states and school districts, and the U.S. Chamber of Commerce and Coopers and Lybrand are working to put this technology into as many places as possible.

Child-Centered Education Funding

Arizona Superintendent of Public Instruction Lisa Keegan described for the Subcommittee the system of education funding she believed to be most child-centered and equitable. While Arizona has not yet implemented such a plan, it is the direction in which they are headed as they comply with a court order to restructure their school finance system. However, the city of Seattle recently announced plans to design a similar funding mechanism for their schools, and the idea, sometimes called "school-based education funding" is rising in prominence among education reformers.

According to Ms. Keegan, education dollars should be "strapped to the back of a child" and follow a child to whichever school he or she attends:

> *Though most assume this is how the system functions, at least within the traditional public schools, I assure you it does not... Very few principals have any control over funds "due" their schools, and worse, have no idea how much money the arrival of a child at their school is worth.*

Ms. Keegan proposed a funding system that essentially sends dollars to the classroom with the child. Such a system would increase equity and access, reduce bureaucracy, and create a true educational marketplace. She called for an end to:

> *... arbitrary and in fact meaningless distinctions between "public" and "charter" and "private" schools...a child is well-served where they can learn, they are not well-served when he or she is in an environment where they can't learn, they are not well-served when they are trapped in any environment where they are doomed to fail.*[89]

A child-centered education funding system would empower parents to make decisions about where their children should attend schools, empower schools receiving the funds to use the money to address the unique needs of their students as efficiently as possible, and to create an accountability system based at the local level. The question of what portion of education dollars reach the classroom would be easily answered: they arrive at the classroom with the child.

The Federal Role

Ensuring that federal education dollars are child centered and spent in the classroom does not necessarily call for an expansion of federal data collection: creating a bureaucracy to track dollars to the classroom would only add to the problem. State and local education agencies can advance accountability by implementing accounting systems that would give taxpayers evidence of where the money is being spent. The role of the federal government is to eliminate ineffective and inefficient education spending and allocate dollars to proven initiatives that make improving education in the classroom their first priority.

---

[89] Testimony of Superintendent Lisa Keegan, *Field Hearing on Education at Crossroads,* , Subcommittee on Oversight and Investigations, Committee on Education and the Workforce, January 31, 1997, No. 105-11.

BEYOND CROSSROADS: WHAT WE LEARNED, THE ROAD AHEAD

The primary purpose of the Crossroads project was to listen and learn in order to make the case for change. Much of what works is simply a matter of common sense. It does not take rocket science to conclude that a good education starts with the family and good instruction. These hearings, however, presented the opportunity to principals, teachers, parents, students and state officials from around the country to share their experiences with what works and what is wasted. Rather than relying on a small, elite group of witnesses who could leave their work to come to Washington and testify, the Subcommittee visited educators, parents and students where learning takes place: the classroom. From small towns to major cities, real people discussed real successes and problems in education. Apart from these hearings, these voices may never have been heard.

Now is the time to act on what we've learned. And the central theme of what we learned is that the federal government cannot consistently and effectively replicate success stories throughout the nation in the form of federal programs. Instead, federal education dollars should support effective state and local initiatives, ensuring that it neither impedes local innovation and control, nor diverts dollars from the classroom through burdensome regulations and overhead.

Reforming the federal role in education is a process that will take time. It has taken thirty years to get to where we are now. However, there are many bold initiatives that Congress can pass to reverse this trend and restore parental and local control over education.

The Federal Role: Supporting What Works

The massive array of federal education programs began as an attempt to address specific problems. Each program received minimal funding at the outset, and most have received additional funds from one year to the next. The current arrangement of federal education funding is as follows: local tax dollars go to Washington, where they are allocated to a variety of purposes, usually to address what someone in the federal government sees as a problem. The money is then returned to states and school districts in the form of categorical programs. This process puts smaller school districts at a disadvantage: States and local school districts are highly dependent on administrators and skilled grant writers to obtain these federal dollars and comply with their requirements, which places a greater burden on poorer and smaller school systems.

It is time to shift the burden of proof of effectiveness to the federal government. If the U.S. Department of Education cannot demonstrate to Congress that a particular program is more effectively spending the money than it would otherwise be spent as part of a general grant, that money should be returned to the states without strings. The largest program, Title I, Aid to Disadvantaged Children, has spent over $100 billion over 30 years with little or no evidence that this program has improved the learning of the children it serves. Congress should ensure that such a waste of funds never happens again.

Return Federal Elementary and Secondary Education Funds to States and Local School Districts

> *Now, if reform is radical simplification, and if we must organize to stop using our teacher's time, our principal's time, our student's time towards initiatives that are not productive to student learning, then your Committee can do this nation a remarkable service if you...end or at least consolidate these programs.*
> --Dr. William Moloney, Commissioner of Education, Colorado

The most comprehensive way to return control of education to parents and school districts is to consolidate all elementary and secondary education funds and send them back to school districts and states in the form of flexible grants. This would shift the balance of power back to parents by facilitating program development and oversight at the local level. Congress could redistribute the funds based on poverty as they are now, but not attach any strings to the dollars.

There are presently several efforts underway to enact legislation that would consolidate certain programs into flexible grants in order to change the federal funding role from being compartmentalized and program-centered to child-centered. Such grants would enable state education agencies, districts and schools to tailor education programs to the unique needs of their students. Accountability and effectiveness would become the focus of federal programs instead of administration and compliance.

Consolidation "Flex" Grants

One immediate avenue Congress can take to send education dollars to the classroom is through consolidating elementary and secondary education programs into flexible grants. Because there are so many small categorical programs, even combining as many as 31 programs, as one plan proposes, only amounts to $2.7 billion. That so many programs spend under $3 billion total is also an argument for consolidating them. Programs could also be consolidated at the discretion of the state, in effect an "optional" grant: Either the legislature or the Governor could decide to receive funds through different federal programs, or as one grant.

Short of implementing a comprehensive education "flex" grant, in the short term, Congress can do the following to put children first andto free states and local school districts from the burdens of unproductive paperwork and regulations.

EMPOWER PARENTS

The federal government can encourage parental involvement in schools by empowering them to be in control of their children's education. The following could facilitate this:

- **Reduce family tax burdens**: Cutting taxes can strengthen families by making it more economically feasible to have one parent home during the day and involved with their child's education during the school day their classroom, or even teaching their child at home. Tax cuts would also free-up income that could be used for tutoring services, summer enrichment programs, school tuition, or other expenses they might choose to incur that would help their child's education.

- **Tax-Free Savings for Education:** Parents are empowered when they have the resources to make decisions that serve the best education interests of their child. Tax credits are a means of providing resources for education without diverting valuable dollars to administrative overhead and bureaucracy and places dollars for education directly into the hands of parents.

  Congress recently passed a bill that accomplishes this - the Parents and Students Savings Account Plus Act. If signed into law this act would allow individuals to contribute up to $2,000 a year per child to an education IRA. Although the contribution would be taxable, interest would accumulate tax-free. Savings in the account could be used for any education-related expense, such as school tuition, books, tutoring, special classes, school uniforms, and transportation costs.

- **Encourage parental choice.** Giving parents the opportunity to choose where they send their children to school gives them more control over the quality of their education. No parent should be forced to send their child to an ineffective, violent or drug-infested school. Although school choice programs should be developed and implemented at the state and local level, school choice can be encouraged at the federal level by empowering low-income families to send their children to effective schools through scholarship programs.

  The implementation of tax-free savings accounts would provide some relief for taxpayers who send their children to alternative schools. Many families with disabled children, or children with behavior or drug problems are sending their children to alternative schools that address the particular needs of specific categories of students. Some of these schools can cost as much as $40,000 a year.

  The House has proposed several pieces of legislation that would provide opportunities specifically for low-income children to escape dangerous or academically failing schools:

  Opportunity Scholarships for students in Washington, D.C.: Led by House Majority Leader Dick Armey, for several years Congress has been unsuccessful in enacting legislation that would provide opportunity scholarships for low-income children in the troubled DC school system. In its current form this proposal would provide $7 million for $3,200 scholarships for about 1,800 low-income students to attend schools of their choice.

  HELP for Poor Children in Failing Schools: Another way to encourage choice for poor children is to allow states to spend federal dollars to create choice programs. Title VI, essentially an education reform block grant, could be vehicle for such a provision. Congressmen Frank Riggs (R-CA) and Jim Talent (R-MO) have introduced legislation that would allow states to create scholarship programs for disadvantaged children living in certain areas using their Title VI block grant dollars.

- **Jump Starts for Charter Schools:** Many charter schools are indefinitely stalled by a lack of capital to start their schools. Leasing or buying buildings for the school can be prohibitively expensive, and charter schools do not often have access to loan or financing options. The federal government currently provides some funds for states to distribute to qualifying charters for start-up costs. In order to expand access to charter schools, Congress should continue its support. In addition, it should not attach strings to the funds and burden them with additional regulations or restrictions or otherwise interfere with their autonomy, and leave to the states entirely how charters should be selected to receive funds.

- **Send Title I to Intended Beneficiaries:** In order to give states true flexibility in providing educational assistance to their disadvantaged students Congress could give states the option to use their Title I program funds to provide direct grants for disadvantaged students. Parents could use these grants for private school tuition or outside tutoring assistance at learning centers.

RETURN CONTROL TO THE LOCAL LEVEL

Expanding local control means reducing the number of decisions about education spending made in Washington. States and local school districts should have the flexibility to allocate funds where they are most needed, and should implement local accountability measures to ensure that the funds will be spent effectively.

Expand Ed-flex flexibility: One way in which Congress could send decision making to the state and local level is to expand the current Ed-flex program to all 50 states and provide for *more* flexibility, such as allowing program funds to be consolidated with other programs.

The Ed-Flex program currently allows only 12 states to issue federal program waivers instead of the Department.[90] This program simplifies the waiver process and enables more school districts to take advantage of available waivers, giving them greater flexibility within federal programs. Many schools are successfully using Ed-Flex to waive the statutory threshold schools must meet in order to implement a school-wide comprehensive reform program with federal Title I funds.[91]

States, however, are not given broad discretion to consolidate federal programs to address one area of particular need. Current waiver authorities cannot waive the requirements that would enable schools to implement truly new and innovative programs. If Congress wants to pass legislation that meets the expectations of increasing flexibility it should allow for states and local school districts to waive more requirements and completely consolidate their federal funds should they desire to do so.

---

[90] The 12 states are: Colorado, Illinois, Iowa, Kansas, Maryland, Massachusetts, Michigan, New Mexico, Ohio, Oregon, Texas and Vermont.
[91] See: U.S. Department of Education, Office of the Inspector General, *State and Local Education Agencies Need More Technical Assistance to Take Full Advantage of the Flexibility Provisions of Title XIV of the Improving America's Schools Act,* ACN: 04-70001, August, 1997.

ENCOURAGE BASIC ACADEMICS

In order to ensure that the federal government does not impede classroom learning by funding ineffective teaching methods and training, it should create criteria and standards for any federally funded research to ensure that any information disseminated by the federal government is based on reliable, replicable research. Research funded by the federal government should be peer-reviewed by disinterested parties before it is distributed, and should meet minimum standards of replicability and statistical significance.

SEND DOLLARS TO THE CLASSROOM

Streamline Federal Education Programs

The Crossroads Project found more than 760 federal education programs. Many of them have similar objectives and the exact same constituency. Even more are small, narrowly tailored programs, many of which were created to serve particular constituencies and special interests and not national education interests. In order to ensure that scarce resources are not spent on small, inefficient programs that only serve narrow constituencies, these programs should be consolidated and the savings sent back to states and local school districts. One way in which this could be done is to consolidate all elementary and secondary education programs that are currently funded at less than $1 million. Currently 56 programs fall below that level.[92]

Eliminate Unfunded Programs

To alleviate the burden of having to keep track of more than one hundred education programs that are no longer funded, and to promote a more efficient system, Chairman Hoekstra introduced the Clean Books Act of 1997. This bill would repeal 69 of the over 100 unfunded programs, including "Education Programs for Commercial Drivers" and "Consumer and Homemaking Education."

Free School Districts to Fund Their Priorities: Increase Federal Funding for Special Education

Congress should do all it can to fulfill its obligation to local school districts to fully fund its share of the mandate placed upon them to provide a free and appropriate education for children, disabled or not. Local school districts are hamstrung by the numerous and expensive requirements in the nation's special education law. Districts are often forced to set aside important general education funding needs to come close to complying with federal requirements.

Reallocating federal funds to special education, without increasing overall education spending, would free-up resources at the local level for general education. In effect this would send more funds to the local level for the classroom, but the funds would remain at the local level in locally designed programs to meet their unique needs and priorities.

---

[92] Based on FY1997 figures.

Reduce the Paperwork Burden

In order to determine what states receive from federal programs for the costs involved in applying for the funds, it is important to know what administrative burden states must fund with their own tax dollars. Most states do not currently track what they must spend of their own funds to receive and comply with federal programs.

The Subcommittee is working, in cooperation with several states, to investigate the extent and cost of the federal paperwork burden. At the direction of the Governor, state education agencies are compiling all the paperwork required by federal education programs and determining the cost of filling out these forms. Such information will enable Congress and the Department to determine how to reduce paperwork and whether the OMB estimates of paperwork burden hours is accurate. In addition, the states participating in this project will be better able to do a cost-benefit analysis of what they receive from federal programs.

As accountability is based more at the state and local level, federal reporting requirements and audits will decrease. This will decrease the paperwork burden and increase resources for instruction.

Hold the Federal Government Accountable: The Results Act

In the past federal programs have placed a low priority on ensuring that their programs are held accountable and actually produce results. To address this serious deficiency in the management of federal programs, Congress passed the Government Performance and Results Act (GRPA) in 1994 in order to require by law that agencies give Congress information by which they can analyze the performance and cost of federal programs. Performance data collected as a result of this legislation will help determine which programs are effective and which should be either eliminated or consolidated into a proven program.

GPRA requires the Department to clearly define their missions, develop long-term goals as well as annual goals, measure their performance by their attainment of these goals, and report to Congress their progress. Under GPRA, the Department is also required to perform program evaluations and use the data to improve their effectiveness.

REFORMING THE FEDERAL ROLE FOR THE 21ST CENTURY

Fifteen years ago, our nation was diagnosed as being at risk - at risk of entering the 21st Century lagging behind other industrialized nations economically and educationally. Since then there has been little evidence of the federal government effectively addressing this problem through its hundreds of duplicative and uncoordinated education programs.

Education policy in this country needs to be re-oriented towards ensuring that children receive a quality education, not preserving programs and bureaucracies. Significant progress needs to be made by all levels of government - solving problems at the federal level is only one component.

The federal government should only play a limited role in education: It should serve education at the state and local level as a research and statistics-gathering agency, disseminating findings and enabling states to share best practices with each other. Local educators must be empowered to teach children with effective methods and adequate resources, without federal interference. Parents must once again be in charge of the education of their children. Schools should be havens for learning, safe from drugs and violence.

Much work remains. It is time for the federal bureaucracy to move out of the way and put children first by supporting what works.

APPENDIX A

Education at a Crossroads
Hearing Witnesses
1995-1998

5/19/95 Washington Irving Elementary School, Chicago, Illinois

Name	Title	Organization
Sister Judith Briselden	Principal	Our Lady of the Gardens Elementary School
Connee Fitch-Blanks	Assistant Director	Chicago Teachers Union Quest Center
Madeleine Maraldi	Principal	Washington Irving Elementary School
Beverly Tunney	Principal	Healey Elementary School
Joe Walsh	representative of	Heartland Institute
Darrell Williams	Scholar	Ameritech
Marvin Wortell	Chairman and Founder	Triton Industries

10/23/95 Learning Enterprise High School, Milwaukee, Wisconsin

Name	Title	Organization
Regina Chesir	Parent	Rufus King for the College Bound
Regis Chesir	Student	Rufus King for the College Bound
Zakiya Courtney	Director	Parents for Choice
Jennifer Evans	Parent	Milwaukee Public Schools
Howard Fuller	Director	Institute for the Transformation of Learning
Pilar Gonzalez	Parent	Milwaukee Public Schools
James Hall	Representative of	Hall, Patterson and Charne
Dan McKinley	President	Partners Advancing Values in Education
Susan Mitchell	President	Mitchell Company
Alex Molnar	Professor	University of Wisconsin-Milwaukee
Antonio Riley	State Representative	Wisconsin State Assembly
Tim Sheehy	President	Milwaukee Chamber of Commerce
Brother Bob Smith	Principal	Messmer High School

1/29/97 New Technology High School, Napa, California

Name	Title	Organization
Marian Bergeson	Secretary for the Governor's Office of Child Development and Education	Office of the Governor of California
Jere Jacobs	Assistant Vice President	Pacific Telesis Group
Ruth McKenna	Chief Deputy Superintendent	Instructional Services (California Dept. Of Education)
Louis Barber	Member	California School Boards Association
Earl Jones	Teacher	George Washington Carver Elementary School
Mark Morrison	Interim Administrator	New Technology High School
Dorothy Erikson	Parent	Santa Rosa, CA
Ruth Workman	Parent	Benicia, CA
Bob Stahl	Parent	Napa County, CA
David Brown	Superintendent	Napa Valley Unified School District
Nancy Todd	Region I Director	Statewide System of School Support

1/30/97 Vaughn Learning Center, San Fernando, California

Name	Title	Organization
Gail Cloud	Parent & Teacher	Riverside, California
Marion Joseph	Member	State Superintendent's Reading Task Force
Steven Baldwin	Member	California State Assembly
Jerry Treadway	Professor of Education	San Diego State University
Carley Ochoa	Director	Special Projects of the Riverside Unified School District
Yvonne Chan	Executive Director	Vaughn Learning Center
Jeannine English	Executive Director	Little Hoover Commission
Jonathan Williams	Co-Director	The Accelerated School
Eric Premack	Director	Charter Schools Project, Institute for Education Reform
Joe Lucente	Principal	Fenton Elementary School

1/31/97 Phoenix City Council Chambers, Phoenix, Arizona

Name	Title	Organization
Lisa Keegan	Superintendent of Public Instruction	Arizona Department of Education
Raymond Jackson	President	ATOP Academy
Karen Butterfield	Executive Director	Flagstaff Arts and Leadership Academy

Patrick Grippe	Assistant Superintendent	Douglas County School District
Jeffrey Flake	Executive Director	Goldwater Institute
B. Kay Lybeck	Teacher	Arizona Education Association
C. Diane Bishop	Education Policy Advisor	State of Arizona
Candie Tapia	Student	Arizona Call-A-Teen Center of Excellence
Mary Ballard	Parent	Arizona Call-A-Teen Center of Excellence
Lois Gerber	Chairman of the Board	National Independent Private Schools Association

3/3/97 Wilmington High School, Wilmington, Delaware

Name	Title	Organization
Thomas Carper	Governor	State of Delaware
Michael Ferguson	Acting Secretary of Education	State of Delaware Department of Public Instruction
George Frunzi	Superintendent	Sussex Vocational Education School District
Lidia Jankowska	Parent	The Charter School
William Manning	President	Red Clay School Board
Peter Rees	Associate Professor of Geography	University of Delaware
Ron Russo	Principal	The Charter School
Tswana Sewell	Student	Wilmington High School
Gavin Standish	Teacher	Coordinator of Instructional Technology,
Michael Stemniski	Teacher	McKean High School
Bob Strong	Principal	Wilmington High School
J. Cameron Yorkston	Assistant Headmaster	The Tatnall School
Rachel Wood	Science Education Specialist	

4/22/97 Blandy Hills Elementary School Milledgeville, Georgia

Name	Title	Organization
Linda Schrenko	State Superintendent	Georgia Dept. Of Education
John Roddy	Director of Federal Programs	Georgia Dept. Of Education
Kelly McCutchen	Executive Director	Georgia Public Policy Foundation
Craig Dowling	Parent and Principal	West Gordon Elementary School
James Mullins	Specialist	Dekalb County School System
Debbie Brooks	Parent	Blandy Hills Elementary

Laura Frederick	Assistant Professor	Georgia State University
Elizabeth Lyons	Principal	C.W. Hill Elementary School
Johnny Isakson	Chairman	Georgia State Board of Education
Gail Hughes	President	Clinch County School District
Buster Evans	Superintendent	Bleckley County School District
Dahlia Wren	Director	Adult Literacy Services, Heart of Georgia Technical Institute
Janet Wes	Former President	Georgia PTA

5/5/97 Cardinal Hayes High School, Bronx, New York

Name	Title	Organization
John O'Connor	Cardinal	Archdiocese of New York
Ninfa Segarra	Deputy Mayor	Office of the Mayor of New York City
Peter Flanegan	Founder	I Have a Dream Program
James Kadamus	Deputy Commissioner for Elementary, Middle, Secondary, and Continuing Education	New York State Dept. Of Education
Joseph Viterity	Professor	New York University
Harold Levy	Chairman	New York City Commission on School Facilities and Maintenance Reform
Bill Andrews	Parent	Parent Information Network
Raymond Domanico	Executive Director	Public Education Association
Noreen Connell	Chairperson	Educational Priorities Panel
Marina Tavarez	Student	Central Park East Secondary School
Paul Schwarz	Co-Director	Central Park East Secondary School
Sharon Ramano	Teacher	WildCat Academy
Pat Kelly	Principal	St. Angela Merici School
Robert Spencer	Student	Cardinal Hayes High School
Linda Morant	Principal	Allen Christian School
Jaclyn Santos	Student	WildCat Academy

5/27/97 Mother of Mercy High School, Cincinnati, Ohio

Name	Title	Organization
Mike Fox	Member	Ohio House of Representatives
John Pennycuff	School Board Member	Winton Woods School District,
Sam Staley	Vice President of Research	Buckeye Institute for Public Policy Solutions

Sandy Wheatley	President	Lakota School District
David Nordyke	Director	Harmony Center
Nancy Schlemmer	Secretary	National PTA
Kathleen Ware	For Michael Brandt Superintendent	Cincinnati Public Schools
Tom Mooney	President	Cincinnati Federation of Teachers
Margaret Gerber	Member	US FIRST Team
Sister Katheryn Ann Connely	Director of Educational Services	Archdiocese of Cincinnati
Nancy Jackson	Former Team Member	US FIRST Team
Cleaster Mims	CEO and President	Marva Collins Preparatory School

5/28/97 Cane Run Elementary School, Louisville, Kentucky

Name	Title	Organization
Anne Northup	Member	U.S. House of Representatives
Diane Price	Teacher	Fern Creek Elementary School & President of the Jefferson County Teachers Association
Joseph Clark	Director for the Division of Program Resources	Kentucky Department of Education
Stephen Daeschner	Superintendent	Jefferson County Public Schools
Libby Marshall	Director of Governmental Relations	Kentucky School Board Association
Sister Amelia Stenger	Director	Archdiocese of Louisville
Edward Reidy	Deputy Commissioner	Kentucky Department of Education
Martin Cothran	Public Policy Analyst	Family Foundation of Kentucky
Carolyn Witt Jones	Director	Partnership for Kentucky Schools
Janet Carrico	President	Kentucky Education Association
Joseph Kelley	Chairman	Kentucky State School Board
Jacqueline Austin	Principal	Kennedy Elementary School

5/29/97 Central High School, Little Rock, Arkansas

Name	Title	Organization
Mike Huckabee	Governor	Arkansas
Elaine Scott	Former Teacher	Little Rock
Mike Watson	President	Arkansas Policy Foundation
Charles Adair	Superintendent	Harrison School District
Edward McKinney	Superintendent	Van Buren School District

Rudolph Howard	Principal	Central High School
Allan Stanford	Member of School Board	Bryant School District
John Riggs	President	Little Rock School Board
Tom Watkins	Principal	Butterfield Junior High School
Dorothy Nayles	Senior Policy Analyst	New Future for Little Rock Youth
Dorothy Welch	Principal	Moody Elementary School

9/12/97 HOPE Central Academy, Cleveland, Ohio

Name	Title	Organization
Thomas Needles	Executive Assistant to the Governor	Office of Gov. George Voinovich
Fannie Lewis	Member	Cleveland City Council
Kenneth Blackwell	Treasurer	State of Ohio
Patrick Sweeney	Member	Ohio State Senate
Davis Brennan	Chairman	The Brennan Group
Bert L. Holt	Director	Cleveland Scholarship and Tutoring Program
Shirley Hawk	Member	Cleveland Board of Education
Ronnie Dunn	Student	Students for Positive Action
Nina Turner	Student	Students for Positive Action
Delvoland Shakespeare	Parent	Our Lady of Peace
Gloria Brown	Parent	Empire Computech School, Collinwood Intermediate School
Irwin Caraballo Sr.	Parent	Luther Memorial School
Mrs. Hoke	Parent	Cleveland
Fred Hoke	Student	Cleveland
Millie Gonzalez	Parent	St. Vitus School
Curtis Gonzalez	Student	St. Vitus School
Adasha Bias	Student	HOPE Central Academy
Pamela Ballard-Hunt	Parent	HOPE Central Academy
Gayle McAngus	Parent	HOPE Tremont Academy
Demetrius Owens	Student	HOPE Central Academy
William Ronschke	Principal	Luther Memorial School
Carol Fawcett	Teacher	Luther Memorial School
Lydia Harris	Retired Principal	St. Adalbert School
Jeanette Polomsky	Principal	St. Vitus School
Nicola Davies	Teacher	St. Vitus School
Sister Hasina Ranee	Administrator	Islamic School of Oasis
Waynee Udovich	Teacher	HOPE Central Academy
Michael Charney	Teacher	Lincoln Middle School

10/2/97 Muskegon Heights Senior High School, Muskegon, Michigan

Name	Title	Organization
John Engler	Governor	State of Michigan
Joanne Emmons	Member	Michigan State Senate
Joe Overton	Vice President	Mackinac Center
Joseph Schulze	Superintendent	Muskegon Public Schools
Gary Scholten	Member	Zeeland School Board
Jim Fisher	President	Fisher Steel and Supply Company
Marvin Nash	Principal	Muskegon Senior High
Thomas Powers	Superintendent	Greater Muskegon Catholic Schools
Jonathan Hoffman		The School Zone
Tom Antioho	Principal	Grand Haven Senior High School
Nathaniel Wells	Bishop	Tri-Valley Charter School
Kevin Megin	Director of Special Education	North Mudkegon Public Schools

11/3/97 East High School, Des Moines, Iowa

Name	Title	Organization
Shery Vanderploeg	Parent	
Ian Binnie	Parent	
Sheri Riley	Miss Iowa	
Amanda DeVan	Student	East High School
Terry Branstad	Governor	State of Iowa
Marvin Pomerantz	Chairman	Iowa Commission on Educational Excellence in the 21st Century
Harold Sandahl	Member	Des Moines Public School Board
Steve McDermott	Principal	Bridgewater Elementary & Fontanelle Jr. High
Ruth Ann Gaines	Iowa Teacher of the Year	East High School
Jim Hawkins	Coordinator	Cooperative Education
Luverne Gubbles	Superintendent	Des Moines Diocesan Schools
Linda Young	Teacher	Des Moines Christian School
Jim Burn	Teacher	Des Moines Christian School
Angela Hasley	Student	Drake
Randy Richardson	Technology Consultant	Loess High Education Agency #13, Council Bluffs

3/20/98 Timnath Elementary School, Ft. Collins, Colorado

Name	Title	Organization
William Moloney	Commissioner of Education	Colorado Dept. of Education
Donald Unger	Superintendent	Poudre R-1 School District
Dan Balcerak	Principal	Timnath Elementary School
Pamela Schmidt	Teacher of the Year	Thunder Ridge Middle School
Randy Everett	Parent & School Board Member	Liberty Common Charter School
Jane Anderson	Parent	Liberty Common Charter School
Richard Schleusener	Parent	Ft. Collins
Tripper Riggs	Student	University of Northern Colorado Lab School
Pat Chase	President	Colorado Association of School Boards
Clair Orr	Member of	Colorado State Board of Education
Bob Selle	Superintendent	East Yuma County School District
Brian McNulty	Assistant Commissioner Office of Special Services	Colorado Dept. of Education

3/30/98 Crossroads Middle School, Lewisberry, Pennsylvania

Name	Title	Organization
Eugene Hickok	Secretary of Education	Pennsylvania Dept. of Education
C. Jack Van Newkirk	Superintendent of Schools	School District of the City of York
Harold Mowery	Vice Chairman	Pennsylvania Senate, Education Committee
Brent Frey	Supervisor of Computer Services	West Shore School District
Sean Duffy	Vice President	The Commonwealth Foundation
Reverand Newman	Grandparent	York
Jennifer Weikert	Parent	McKinley Elementary School
Ben Jenkins	Student	Crossroads Middle School
Erin McConnell	Student	Crossroads Middle School
Matt Knickman	Student	Crossroads Middle School

Hearings in Washington, DC

3/6/97 Washington, DC Crossroads Project "Kick Off" Hearing

Name	Title	Organization
Lamar Alexander	Former Governor & US Secretary of Education	Tennessee
Deliane Easton	Superintendent of Public Instruction	California

5/1/97 Washington DC Joint Hearing on "What Works and What is Wasted in the District of Columbia School System?"

Name	Title	Organization
Julius Becton	Chief Executive Officer	DC Public Schools
Joyce Ladner	Member	DC Financial Responsibility and Management Assistance Authority
Bruce Maclaury	Chairman	DC Public Schools Emergency Board of Trustees
Don Reeves	President	DC Board of Education
Kevin Chavous	Chairman	Committee on Education, Libraries and Recreation, DC City Council
Marion Barry	Mayor	District of Columbia
Delabian L. Rice-Thurston		Parents United for DC Public Schools
Judith Jones	Parent of former DCPS student	Charter School Activist
Tara Pickstock	Senior	Bannekar High School

5/8/97 Washington DC Hearing on "Dollars to the Classroom"

Name	Title	Organization
Christine Olson	Policy Analyst for Domestic Policy	Heritage Foundation
Barbara Stock Nielsen	State Superintendent of Education & Chief Executive Officer for the State Department of Education	State of South Carolina
Charles Garris	Superintendent	Unionville-Chadds Ford School District
Helen Martin	Teacher	Unionville High School

6/24/97 Washington, DC Hearing on "What Works and What is Wasted in Federal Drug Violence Prevention Programs?"

Name	Title	Organization
Joe Barton	Member	US House of Representatives
Bob Etheridge	Member	US House of Representatives
Carlotta Joyner	Director	Education and Employment Issues, GAO
Eric Voth	representative of	International Drug Strategy Institute
Lawrence Sherman	Professor	Dept. Of Criminology and Criminal Justice, University of Maryland
Cyril Wantland	Director	Safe and Drug Free Schools, Jefferson City Public Schools, Kentucky

7/8/97 Washington DC Hearing on "What Works and What is Wasted in Teacher Training Programs"

Name	Title	Organization
Robert Seabrooks	Deputy Assistant General for Audits	US Dept. Of Education
Andrew Zucker	Program Manager	Science and Mathematics Education, SRI International
Daniel Kasprzyk	Program Director	School and Staffing Survey, National Center for Education Statistics, US Dept. Of Education
Stephen Bohrer	Superintendent	U.S.D. #462, Kansas
Lynn Coffin	Senior Director	Center for Innovation, National Education Association

7/31/97 Washington DC Full Committee Hearing on Literacy: A Review of Current Federal Programs

Name	Title	Organization
Maris Vinovskis	Professor of History	University of Michigan
Herbert Walberg	Research Professor of Education and Psychology	University of Illinois at Chicago
Joe Johnson, Jr.	Director of the Collaborative for School Improvement	Charles A. Dana Center, University of Texas at Austin
Cheryl Wilhoyte	Superintendent	Madison Metropolitan School District, Wisconsin
Andy Hayes	Department of Educational Design and Management	University of North Carolina at Wilmington

APPENDIX B

A Survey of Local School Superintendents

July 17, 1996

Dear Superintendent,

The goal of this survey is to assess, in a rudimentary way, the impact of federal education policies and regulations on the activities of local education agencies. To do this, we are requesting information from you on the profile of your district and on the sources and uses of your federal education funds. In addition, we are requesting background information on the costs related to federal regulations, mandates (funded and unfunded), and requirements tied to federal program participation.

While some of the information requested in this survey is very specific, please do not go beyond readily available information to complete this survey. If the requested data is not readily available, either provide a "best guess" estimate of the statistic, or simply skip the question. Please feel free to elaborate on any section, or to provide additional comments to the survey as you see fit.

Thank you in advance for your assistance in this very important project. If you have any questions, please feel free to contact the individuals listed on the cover of this survey.

Sincerely,

PETE HOEKSTRA
Chairman,
Subcommittee on Oversight
and Investigations

DISTRICT PROFILE:

Enrollment in 1995-96 School Year

    Total………………………………………………..….. _____

    Average Daily Attendance……………………….. _____

    Percent Minority Students……………………….. _____

    Percent Eligible for Free or Reduced Lunch…….. _____

Personnel in 1995-96 School Year (in FTEs)

    School District Administrative Staff (total)……... _____

        # Superintendents………………………….. _____

        # Assistants to Superintendents…………… _____

        # Instruction Coordinators…………………. _____

        # Other District Staff……………………… _____

    Instructional Staff (total)………………………… _____

        # Principals……………………………….. _____

        # Assistant Principals……………………… _____

        # Teachers………………………………… _____

        # Aides……………………………………... _____

        # Librarians………………………………... _____

        # Guidance Counselors……………………. _____

        # Other Instructional Staff………………... _____

Support Staff (total)... _____

 # Secretaries and Clerical Support............ _____

 # Transportation................................ _____

 # Food Services................................. _____

 # Physical Plant Support...................... _____

 # Health and Recreation...................... _____

 # Other Support Staff......................... _____

Facilities:

 # Elementary Schools.............................. _____

 # Middle Schools................................... _____

 # High Schools..................................... _____

 Other (child care, administrative, etc.).............. _____

Budget for Most Recent Year Available: **School Year** _____

 Total Revenue... _____

  Federal (total)............................... _____

   Chapter I/Title I....... .... _____

   Eisenhower Math and Science...... _____

   Children with Disabilities............ _____

   Safe and Drug Free Schools......... _____

   Impact Aid............................. _____

   Bilingual Education................... _____

   Indian Education...................... _____

   Chapter II (Block Grant)............ _____

   Vocational Education................ _____

   Other (Nutrition, Demo, Grants, etc.) _____

State (total).................................. _____

    State School Lunch Program...... _____

Local (total)................................... _____

    Tax (Property)......................... _____

    Contributions.......................... _____

    Lunch Fees............................. _____

    Transportation Fees.................. _____

    Other..................................... _____

Total Expenditures............................ _____

    Instruction............................... _____

    Operation and Maintenance......................... _____

    Food Service............................ _____

    Capital Outlay.......................... _____

    Interest on Debt........................ _____

    Other..................................... _____

Title I

    Total Grant.............................. _____

    Amount that went to:

    Teachers Salaries........................... _____

    Instructional Aides......................... _____

    Instructional Materials and Equipment... _____

    Administration (salaries and expenses)... _____

    Other Professional Salaries................. _____

    Other Expenses............................. _____

Eisenhower Math and Science

    Total Grant………………………………….. _____

        Teachers Salaries……………………….. _____

        Instructional Aides……………………….. _____

        Instructional Materials and Equipment…. _____

        Administration (salaries and expenses)… _____

        Other Professional Salaries……………… _____

        Other Expenses………………………….. _____

IDEA

    Total Grant…………………………………… _____

        Teachers Salaries……………………….. _____

        Instructional Aides……………………….. _____

        Instructional Materials and Equipment…. _____

        Administration (salaries and expenses)… _____

        Other Professional Salaries……………… _____

        Other Expenses………………………….. _____

Safe and Drug Free Schools

    Total Grant……………………………………. _____

        Teachers Salaries……………………….. _____

        Instructional Aides……………………….. _____

        Instructional Materials and Equipment…. _____

        Administration (salaries and expenses)….. _____

        Other Professional Salaries……………… _____

        Other Expenses…………………………… _____

PAPERWORK AND REPORTING REQUIREMENTS

Paperwork and Reporting

Total Estimated Number Of Forms
    Filed Each Year............................. _____

Number Submitted to the Federal
    Government.................................. _____

Number Submitted to the State............... _____

Number of State Forms tied to
    Federal Programs........................... _____

Number of Mandatory or
    Near-Mandatory Forms.................... _____

If possible, please submit your district's completed application for the following federal programs and provide an estimate of the resources (staff time, fees for grant writer, copying, postage, etc.) utilized in completing the application. Also include an estimate of the resources expended meeting the various reporting requirements of each program and the size of the final award.

Safe and Drug Free Schools

Estimated Cost to Complete Application/Plan...... _____

Estimated Cost to Complete Required Reports.... _____

Size of Final Grant...................................... _____

Title I

Estimated Cost to Complete Application/Plan...... _____

Estimated Cost to Complete Required Reports..... _____

Size of Final Grant...................................... _____

Eisenhower Professional Development

    Estimated Cost to Complete Application/Plan...... _____

    Estimated Cost to Complete Required Reports...... _____

    Size of Final Grant...................................... _____

IDEA

    Estimated Cost to Complete Application/Plan...... _____

    Estimated Cost to Complete Required Reports...... _____

    Size of Final Grant...................................... _____

Impact Aid

    Estimated Cost to Complete Application/Plan...... _____

    Estimated Cost to Complete Required Reports...... _____

    Size of Final Grant...................................... _____

Indian Education

    Estimated Cost to Complete Application/Plan...... _____

    Estimated Cost to Complete Required Reports...... _____

    Size of Final Grant...................................... _____

Bilingual Education

    Estimated Cost to Complete Application/Plan...... _____

    Estimated Cost to Complete Required Reports...... _____

    Size of Final Grant...................................... _____

Please include a list of other federal education programs for which your district applied and the grant amounts received (discretionary grant programs). What is the estimated cost of applying for these programs? Please try to separate out the estimated cost for applications that were not funded.

OTHER GRANTS

Name of Grant…………………………..……….. _____

Estimated Cost to Complete Required Reports…… _____

Estimated Cost to Complete/Plan..………...…….. _____

Size of Final Grant……………………………….. _____

REGULATIONS

In addition to program rules and regulations, many education programs require assurances of broader federal regulatory compliance before federal grants can be provided. The bulk of the regulatory costs are due to laws pertaining to *accessibility* (ADA, IDEA, and the Rehabilitation Act), *asbestos* (Asbestos Hazard Emergency Response Act), *lead in paint and drinking water* (Lead Contamination Control Act), *underground storage tanks* (Resource Conservation and Recovery Act), and *radon*. Finally, the National School Board Association has repeatedly testified that the *Davis-Bacon Act*, which requires the payment of federally determined prevailing wages on federally-funded construction, inflates the cost of school construction.

Please provide any available information you may have concerning the added costs of federal regulations on the operation of your district. If no information is available, please comment on your "sense" of the cost, the usefulness of the regulations, and any insights into whether these regulations could be simplified, eliminated or left to the states.

PROGRAM EVALUATION

While various evaluations are performed on federal education programs, it would be helpful to get an "in the trenches" view of the successful aspects of these programs, as well as any problems stemming from either the operation or administration of federal programs. Please provide any comments you may have concerning federal programs for which you have received funding (Chapter I, Safe and Drug Free Schools, Eisenhower Professional Development, Bilingual Education, IDEA, etc.).

What are the greatest barriers your district faces in providing all your students a high quality education?

How have federal education programs contributed to your local education goals?

How have federal education programs detracted from your local education goals?

Ideally, how would your district like to use federal education funds, assuming they were provided in a single block grant, or in a more flexible funding stream?

What are the greatest benefits, cost or otherwise, to participation in federal education programs?

How does your district integrate Federal education programs into your regular instruction program?

How well have federal officials met your needs for information and flexibility with regard to Federal education programs? (e.g. Did the Department of Education communicate with you in a timely manner regarding program regulations? Do they respond promptly to any questions or concerns? Have they worked with your district to enable you to use federal programs in a way which best serves your local goals?)

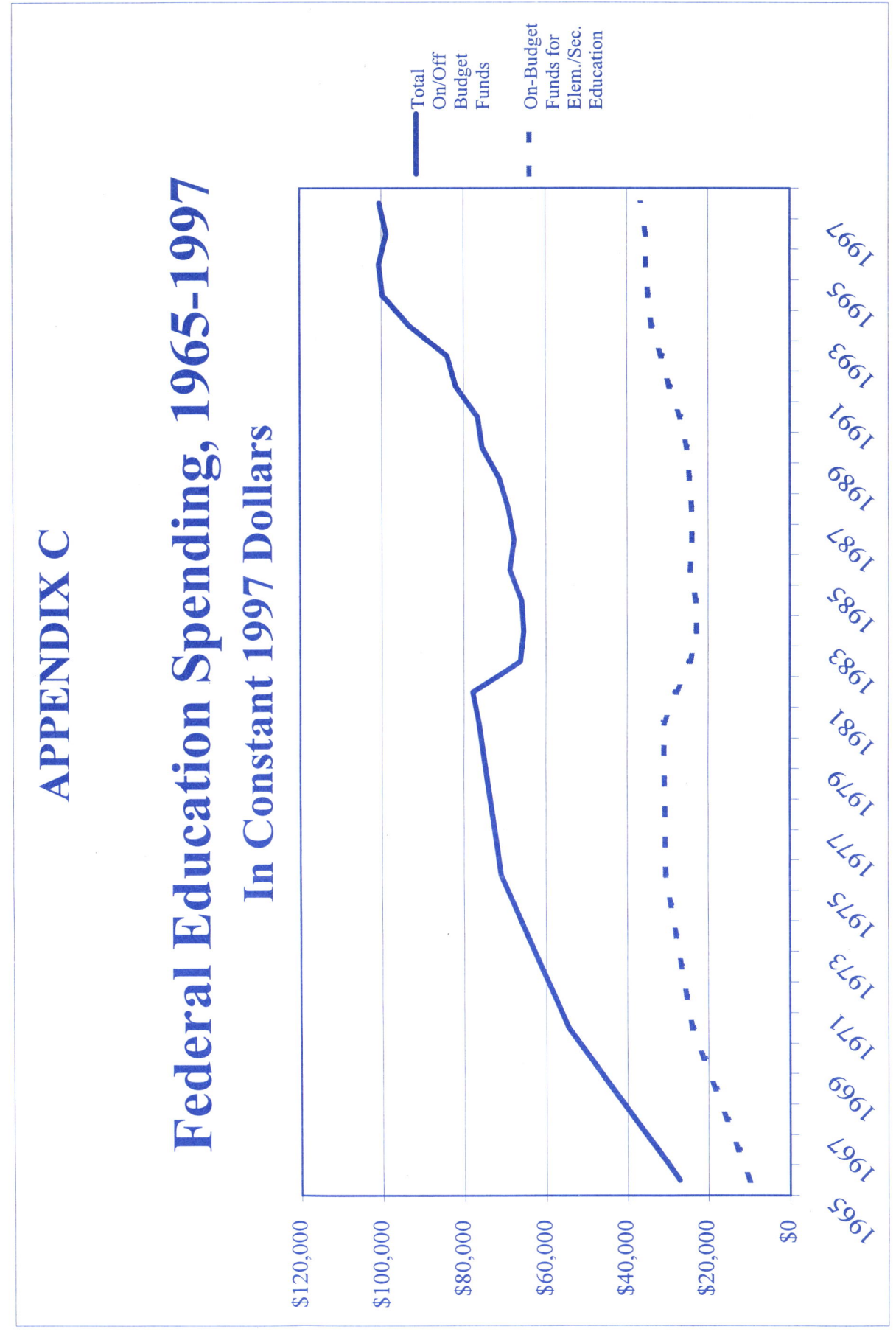

Appendix D

Crossroads Project Cost Disclosures

The following are the expenses incurred from 1995 to 1998 by Republicans and Democrats for field hearings and other activities for the Crossroads Project.

Year	Republican	Democrat	Total
1995	$3,015.54	$1,135.78	**$4,151.32**
1996	$4,226.82	$1,135.78	**$5,362.60**
1997	$17,657.64	$7,872.11	**$25,529.75**
1998	$3,771.27	$1,232.47	**$5,003.74**
Total	**$28,671.27**	**$11,376.14**	**$40,047.41**

APPENDIX E

INTERESTING FACTS AND FIGURES ON THE FEDERAL ROLE IN EDUCATION

Total Number of Federal Education Programs	788
Number of Agencies, Department, Boards, and Commissions Administering Federal Education Programs	40
Total FY 97 Funding	$96,869,343,420
Number of Department of Education Programs	307 (38%)
Funding for Department of Education Programs	$59,000,000,000 (61%)
Largest Funded Program on List	Federal Family Educational Loans (FFEL): PLUS Loans $17,700,000,000
Smallest Funded Program on List	Smithsonian Tropical Research Institute $20,000 *Program Description: To fund one federal employee who administers the outreach program which interacts with local schools about the tropical research being performed in the San Blas, Panama, area.*
The Department of Education, USDA, and HHS make up	84% of the total funding 64% of the total programs
K-12 programs and Post-secondary programs make up	56% of the total programs

CATEGORY BREAKDOWNS

Category	Programs	Percent of Programs
CONSTRUCTION	9	1%
GENERAL EDUCATION	52	7%
EDUCATION RESEARCH	14	2%
K-12	181	23%
LIBRARIES	9	1%
PROFESSIONAL DEVELOPMENT & TEACHER TRAINING	60	8%
POSTSECONDARY	259	33%
PRESCHOOL	17	2%
RESEARCH	27	3%
SOCIAL SERVICES	42	5%
TRAINING	79	10%
SET ASIDE	6	1%

Minority Views

CROSSROADS HEARINGS: A REPUBLICAN ASSAULT ON PUBLIC EDUCATION

I. Introduction

For the past 18 months, the Oversight and Investigations Subcommittee held 18 oversight hearings under the umbrella of "Education at a Crossroads: What Works and What's Wasted". The Majority had a predetermined agenda that it sought witnesses to verify or validate; they refused to allow the Minority to call sufficient numbers of witnesses to have a truly balanced record.

This staged education road-show—with its preordained agenda to discredit federal aid to education and undermine the Department of Education –failed to make a single recommendation to improve public education. Rather than engaging in objective, bipartisan fact-finding, the Majority repeatedly stacked the hearings to promote their political agenda. The Republican report reflects little of what their own witnesses said during hearings.

During each Crossroads hearing, the Majority dictated the subject matter, selected the witnesses, and structured the panels, without consultation or involvement of the Minority. The Majority limited the Minority to one witness per panel with a 5 or 6 to 1 Majority- to- Minority witness ratio. A total of 189 majority witnesses were selected by the Republican Majority with the Democratic Minority being allowed only 26.[1]

Rather than seek testimony on programs and proposals that boost student achievement, enhance teacher performance, address crumbling and overcrowded schools, and improve

---

[1] See Appendix 1

technology in the schools, the Majority stacked the hearings with people they sought out to support their preordained conclusions.

In truth, the Crossroads hearings were orchestrated to discredit local administrators of public schools and minimize the value and use of federal dollars by falsely suggesting too few dollars from federal programs go to the classroom. Since the Republicans took control of the House of Representatives in 1994, they have engaged in an unsubstantiated, untrue, and unrelenting assault on federal aid to public education. The Republicans have proposed:

- *Abolishing the Department of Education.*
- *Diverting billions of dollars in public school funds for private school vouchers*
- *Cutting school lunches*
- *Block-granting Title I education programs, thus abolishing program accountability and targeting to poor students*
- *Ending equal opportunity in higher education*
- *Gutting bilingual education*
- *Tax cuts for the wealthy to send children to private schools*
- *Slashing billions of dollars from education programs*
- *Eliminating the summer youth jobs program*
- *Eliminating school-to-work opportunities for high school students*
- *Eliminating the in-school interest subsidy for student loans*
- *Eliminating the safe and drug-free school program*

The Republican Majority's legislative platform fails to support America's public school children, its parents, teachers, and community leaders to meet unprecedented challenges facing public schools. Today, K-12 enrollments are increasing at record rates. Public schools face a $112 billion school building crisis to address crumbling and overcrowded schools. Class sizes remain unacceptably high, and schools are facing more children for whom English is a second language. The Majority Crossroads Report not only attempts to undermine the federal/state partnership in education, it ignores these critical priorities. The Majority has squandered a key opportunity to provide leadership on renewing our nation's public schools and enhancing educational opportunities for all Americans. "What's Wasted" is valuable time the Majority had to create a positive record of support for public education which the public is demanding of the federal government and which stands out as our greatest national responsibility.

II. False Attacks on Education

1. MYTH: *Over 788 Federal education programs directly impact elementary and secondary education*

The Crossroads Report is designed to weaken the nation's public schools by propagating myths, distortions, misconceptions, and outright lies about the federal-state education partnership.

Last year, the Majority falsely claimed time and time again, that there were 788 federal education programs.[2] It has consistently been in the context of problems with K-12 education in America, leaving the clear impression that those 788 programs are aimed at addressing K-12

---

[2] Representative Hoekstra stated that he sought and received confirmation of the list from the Congressional Research Service (CRS): "Is this an accurate list of government's involvement in education? And they said it is accurate..." (Congressional Record, March 19, 1996). However, in a memorandum from CRS to the Education Committee Majority, February 15, 1997, CRS stated: other than looking for expired authorizations, we have not questioned whether programs categorized as being education-related by OMB in CFDA actually are, or are not, education-related. Determination of whether a program supports education may be judgmental or arbitrary.

education needs. An examination of the 788 list[3] shows it has little relationship to K-12 education. The list includes some 33 research and training programs within the Department of Agriculture, none designed for elementary and secondary students, and are not "education programs" by any reasonable stretch.

The National Oceanic Administration, which deals with the study of pollution and management and resources of our marine environment, is listed with 16 "education programs". The collection of data, or research, or similar items do not belong on a K-12 education list.

The Department of Defense has 20 programs listed in this document, dealing with research activities that the DOD conducts: information gathering, information disseminating, training programs within the Defense Department. They are not K-12 education programs.

The Energy Department has 22 items listed. The Department of Health and Human Services has 169 programs listed in this document, that range from child welfare programs, substance abuse, AIDS prevention programs, programs for diabetes, and all of the Centers for Disease Control programs of research; these programs are important, but they are not K-12 education programs.

This list of "education programs" also includes: 60 medical research grant programs in NIH; 12 nutrition programs; military training; billions of dollars in disaster relief; and scores of other programs such as the "Boat Sludge Educational Grant Program," and the "Air Transportation Centers of Excellence Program."

The truth is the 788 programs include:

      183 are no longer authorized or funded;
      139 are postsecondary or adult education programs;
       71 fund special research;

---

[3] See Appendix 2

    68 provide employment or job-related training and technical assistance;
    58 are for the education and training of health professionals;
    47 provide public information or community outreach;
    27 support the arts, museums, or historic preservation;
    26 provide various services to individuals;
    16 fund construction projects, community development, and community service; and
    11 are nutrition programs.

Of the 305 programs identified as Department of Education programs, 122 are unauthorized, unfunded, or simply non-existent. Of the remaining 183 Department of Education programs pertaining to pre-K through postgraduate education and training, only 102 programs impact elementary and secondary education. Crossroads exaggerated its relevance to 788 "programs". The reality is there are only 102 K-12 education programs

Notwithstanding correspondence from Secretary Riley to Chairman Goodling that refutes the 788 federal education programs, and notwithstanding a GAO[4] report indicating that only 10[5] programs administered by the Department of Education are aimed specifically at K-12 education, the Republican Majority continues to propagate the 788 federal education myth.

Ignoring the truth, the Majority has continued to use this inflated list to suggest inefficient duplication of federal programs and excessive federal bureaucracy. In fact the Clinton administration has worked with Congress to strengthen our education programs.

- Through the 1993 National Performance Review, the Clinton Administration has worked to eliminate unnecessary and ineffective programs. Through Fiscal Year 1997, the Department proposed to eliminate, phase-out, or consolidate more than 100 programs.

---

[4] See Federal Education Funding: Multiple Programs and Lack of Data Raise Efficiency and Effectiveness Concerns (GAO/T-HEHS-98-46, Nov. 6, 1997).
[5] See Appendix 3

- The Department of Education administers more dollars per employee than any other Cabinet-level agency. Currently, 98 cents of every appropriated dollar goes to states, schools, and students.

2. *MYTH: Lack of Accountability on Programs' Effectiveness*

The Republican Majority charges that the effectiveness of federal education programs are seldom measured, particularly Title I. The Majority's report states that "billions of dollars are spent on programs where even the most basic information on effectiveness is lacking". The fact is that every two years the Department of Education issues the "Biennial Evaluation Report" which contains an assessment of programs administered by the Department. In addition to information on goals, objectives, and strategic initiatives, the report summarizes evaluation findings on what helps program participants to increase their achievement and improve their performance.

In response to research indicating that closing the achievement gap between disadvantaged students and their more advantaged peers had stalled, the 1994 reauthorization of Title I implemented several monitoring requirements designed to promote student improvement. The Department also developed a plan to link Title I program objectives to specific indicators to assess whether program objectives are met. For instance the objective to have well-qualified teachers and aides serve low-achieving students was linked to increased training and credentialing of teachers and aides. The Department also commissioned more than a dozen studies[6] to be used in achieving its overall objectives to help disadvantaged children meet high standards.

---

[6] See Appendix 4

Title I is a perfect example of how the Department's use of evaluations play an important role in strengthening a program. However, the Republican Majority's emphasis on block granting, eliminating oversight, and eliminating paperwork, flies in the face of the kinds of assessments that the Majority purport to want. The reality is that assessments are not possible without information.

3. MYTH: Too little is going to the classroom because of bloated bureaucracy

In furtherance of their agenda to undermine federal education programs, the Republicans falsely claim that the Department of Education and the programs the Department operates are gobbling up funds for often wasteful administrative purposes rather than targeting dollars to the classroom. The Majority has falsely claimed that 35 to 40 cents of every federal education dollar "get sucked up into the bureaucracy and paperwork".

There is no truth to this demagoguery. In fact, less than 2% of the Department of Education's budget is spent on federal administrative costs.[7] The remaining 98% of the Department's budget is sent out to states, school districts, and local communities. In addition, nearly all major elementary and secondary education programs include a 5% cap on funds that may be used by state and local educators for administrative purposes and for program coordination, evaluation, and technical assistance.[8]

The most disturbing theme of this false mantra is the incipient condemnation of state and local officials "wasting" federal moneys and not getting "dollars to the classroom". Their theme

---

[7] Indeed, the Department has the lowest administrative overhead of the 14 cabinet agencies, with only one employee for every $7 million in budget authority.
[8] See Appendix 5

is that notwithstanding the fact that only 2% is kept in the federal bureaucracy and 98% of federal funds go out to the states, only 65% get to the classroom. In fact, understanding where education dollars go at the local level has been limited by a lack of detailed data that is consistent across school districts. Frankly, we do not believe this is our business, and abhor this interference into local affairs. We believe it is enough for the "feds" to make sure their own bureaucratic expense stays at 2%, and the states stays at 5%. For instance, the determination of whether an expense is classified as administrative or instructional varies from one school district to another. Some schools classify teacher aides and professional development as administrative, while others classify them as instructional. Recently, Coopers & Lybrand developed a financial analysis model that provides a source of detailed information on where the education dollar goes, including how much money reaches the school level and how much is used for instruction, professional development, administration, and other functions. The model is being implemented in 2 states (South Carolina and Rhode Island) and several dozen school districts in other states. Based on 1995-96 data provided by the state of South Carolina for 33 school districts and by the Milwaukee Public Schools, this accounting system shows that:

- In Milwaukee, 90% of all Title I funds were spent at the school level. Information on the share of Title I funds spent at the school and district levels is being obtained for the South Carolina districts, but the similar percentages spent on instruction and instructional support in both areas suggest that the school share in South Carolina will be similar to that in Milwaukee.

- Although Milwaukee and the South Carolina districts used their Title I funds in somewhat different ways, they spend the same proportion of their funds (93%) on instruction and instructional support. Over three-fourths of the Title I money was spent on direct instruction (77-78%), and an additional 15-16% went for instructional support.

The real reason too few dollars are going to classroom is because we are underinvesting in education at all levels of government. In particular, the federal share of education funding has declined. Since 1980, the federal share of elementary and secondary spending decreased from 13% to 7.8%. In higher education, the reduction was 18.0% to 11.9%.

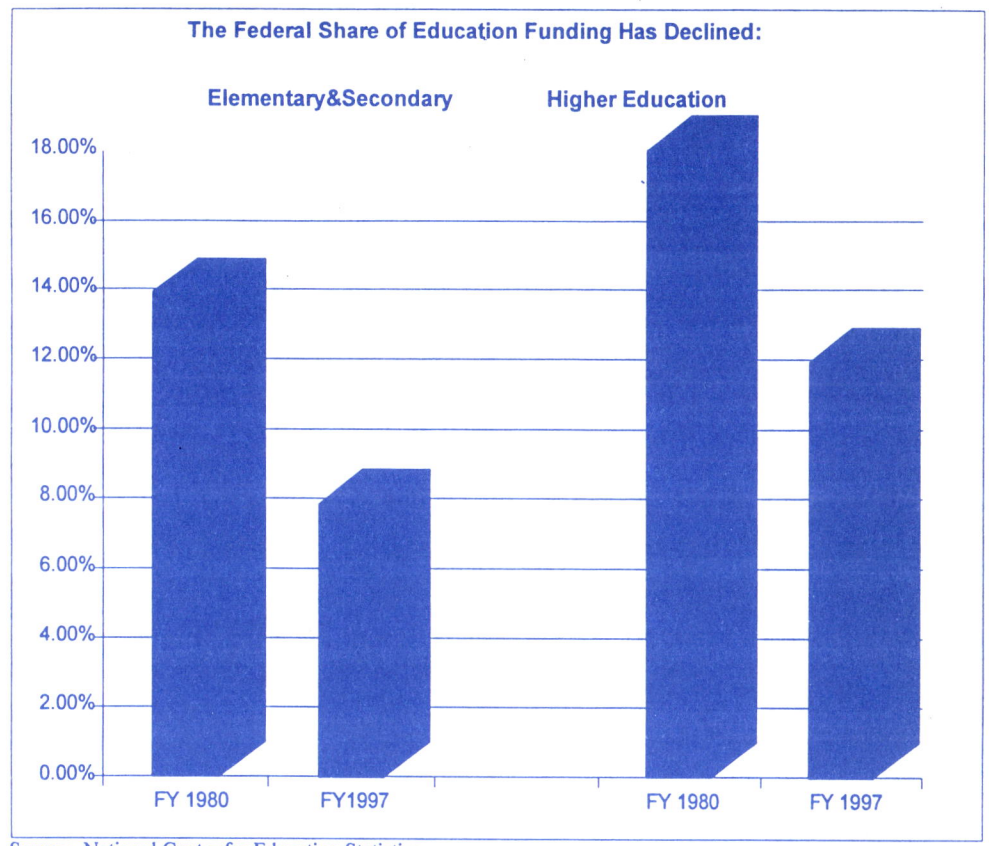

Source: National Center for Education Statistics

In fact, the Department of Education makes up only 1.8% of the 1998 federal budget, down from 2.5% in the mid-eighties (see chart below). These reductions are occurring in the face of record level enrollments in K-12 and higher education; increased number of students with disabilities being served in federal programs; and more children having difficulty speaking English.

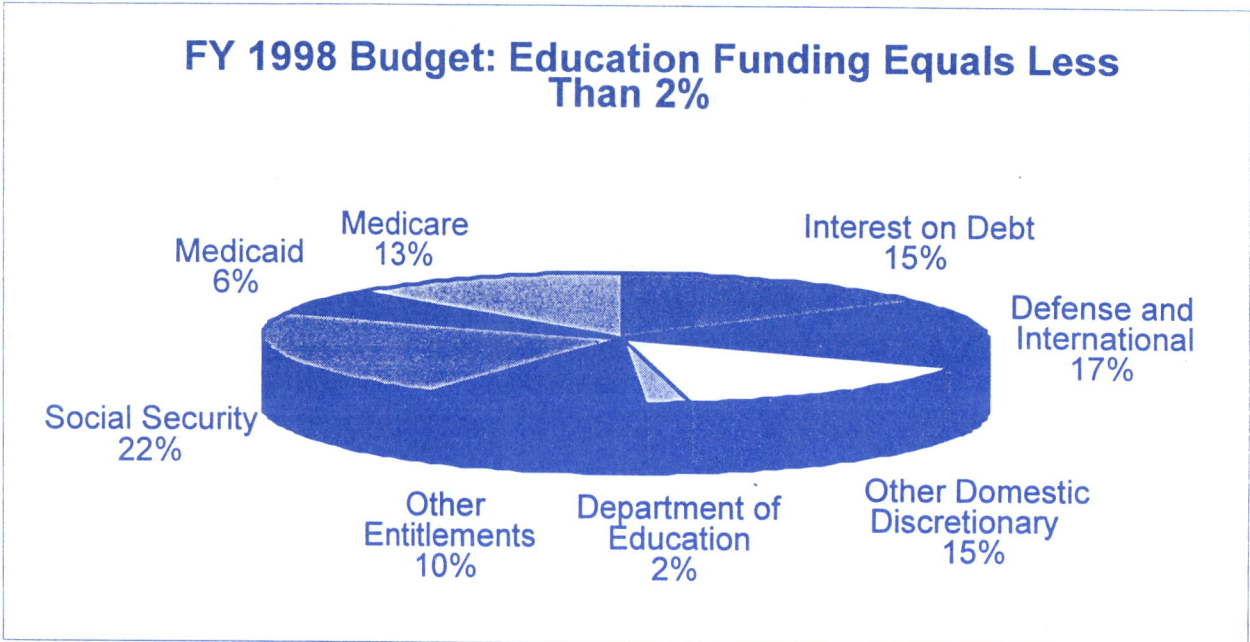

Source: NEA, based on CBO and Department of Education data (totals do not add due to rounding)

According to recent national polls, well over half the public believes we are investing too little in education; 75% of the public supports using federal budget surplus funds for education. We will only succeed in bringing more dollars to the classroom when we are committed to increasing our investments in our neighborhood schools and communities.

4. *MYTH: The Department of Education is bureaucratic and inflexible*

In fact, current law provides broad authority that gives parents, teachers, school administrators, and school districts greater control over how federal education dollars are spent. Under this Education Flexibility Partnership Demonstration Program (Ed-Flex) state education agencies and school districts can now get waivers[9] exempting them from federal requirements in order to improve schools and raise the academic achievement of students.

---

[9] Under the waiver authorities in the Elementary and Secondary Education Act (ESEA), the Goals 2000: Educate America Act and the School-to-Work Opportunities Act, school districts, state education agencies and states may request waivers from particular federal requirements that impede efforts to increase student achievement. These three education laws and the Job Training Partnership Act (JTPA) give the U.S. Secretaries of Education and Labor

The following are examples of waivers that have been approved by the Secretary, and which are representative of the types of waivers an Ed-Flex State might consider in order to improve teaching and learning for its students:

The Fort Worth, Texas School District received a waiver allowing it to target an extra portion of its Title I dollars to four high-poverty, inner-city elementary schools. The schools were chosen for a complete overhaul due to low achievement on the Texas Assessment of Academic Skills (TAAS) and other factors. Each school uses Title I funds to improve instruction for all its students and is reorganizing staff, lengthening the school year, enhancing instruction in reading and math, providing extensive teacher training, and strengthening links to the community.

Montgomery County Schools in Troy, North Carolina received a waiver permitting Troy Elementary School to implement a school-wide program even though the percentage of children from low-income families at the school (45.75%) is slightly below the statutory minimum poverty threshold required for school-wide programs. The school has undergone extensive planning to implement its school-wide program, which promotes the integration of resources and emphasizes continual assessments of students' progress.

As part of Oregon's comprehensive school improvement efforts, the Oregon Department of Education received a waiver of certain requirements of the Carl D. Perkins Vocational and Applied Technology Education Act. The waiver a allows consortia of school districts and community colleges, based on Oregon's workforce development regions, to qualify for and receive Federal funds under the Perkins Act. The waiver also enables small community colleges

---

the ability to waive requirements in both statutory and regulatory requirements of JTPA and many federal elementary and secondary education programs.

to join these consortia by allowing all participating institutions in a consortium to contribute to the $50,000 the law otherwise requires each postsecondary institution to contribute. The consortia will use the Perkins funds to strengthen vocational education programs for both high school and postsecondary school students.

III. What Works: Strong Support for Federal Education Funding

Despite the Majority's repeated attempts to exclude witnesses who support a strong federal-state education partnership, the subcommittee did hear from witnesses who thought the federal government's role in education is not only effective, but indispensable. Large numbers of disadvantaged public school children depend on federal assistance, from school lunches to bilingual education to the education of children with disabilities and other programs. Witnesses recounted that the federal government became involved in education because of the failure of many states and communities to appropriately educate their citizenry. A witness at the Des Moines, Iowa hearing testified that over the past twenty years it was the federal government that insisted disabled children receive an education. Prior to the federal involvement local school districts did nothing to educate the disabled. She recalled that disabled children were excluded from all educational programs and either educated in basements or expelled from schools.[10]

At a Crossroads hearing in Washington, D.C., Delain Eastin, the Superintendent of Public Instruction for the State of California pointed out that education is a national priority because of its importance in developing an informed and responsible citizenry as the foundation of a strong

---

[10] Before the Individuals with Disabilities Education Act was enacted in 1975, P.L. 94-142, more than 1 million children with disabilities were denied an education in America's public schools. IDEA began a partnership among federal, state, and local governments, and with families and teachers to reach a national goal: educating children with disabilities. Today, more than 5.8 million school-age children exercise their right to a free, appropriate education in the public schools.

economy and the national defense. She expressed unqualified support for a strong and continuous federal role in public education.

Other witnesses, like Ruth McKenna, Chief Deputy Superintendent for Instructional Services in California, and Elaine Scott, former Chairperson of the Arkansas State Board of Education, testified in support of "a very strong role for the federal government" to improve education at the state and local levels. Both McKenna and Scott testified that federal dollars have dramatically closed the gap between rich and poor schools in some states. Testimony of these witnesses was confirmed in a January 1998, report of the General Accounting Office. That report, entitled "School Finance: State and Federal Efforts to target Poor Students", made the following conclusions: "Federal funding was more targeted to poor students than state funding in 45 of 47 states. On average, for every $1 of federal funding districts received for each student, they received an additional $4.73 in federal funding per poor student. In general, the greater federal targeting had the effect of raising the additional funding for poor students from the state-only average of $.62
to a combined state and federal average of $1.10, a 77-percent increase. This increase reflects that most states' relatively small share of federal funds was highly targeted."

Over the 18 month period we learned that the role of the federal government is indispensable in helping to effectuate local school reform. At a subcommittee hearing in New York, Paul Schwarz, Co-Director, of the Central Park East Secondary School testified that Goals 2000 funds have served to develop a teaching mentoring program which helps teachers' assistants become certified teachers, which, in turn, serves to address the shortage of minority teachers in New York City public schools. Schwarz also discussed how federal challenge grants for technology were being used in New York City public schools to develop digital libraries in schools, new multimedia curriculum content, and wide area networking to link learning resources across schools.

In Cincinnati, Nancy Schlemmer, Secretary of the National Parent Teachers Association, stated that federal Title I and Eisenhower Professional Development funds have allowed Cincinnati to shape its education reform efforts by developing stronger connections between schools and families, higher standards for curriculum, improvements for professional development, and improvements in teaching and educational choices for families and students. More specifically, Cincinnati Public Schools use Eisenhower Professional Development funds to help math and science teachers align their own practices with nationally recognized standards. Additionally, Title I funds are used in the "Three Plus Program." This program helps students who are more than two years over age for the third grade receive intensive academic support in order to advance to their age appropriate grade. Another local program, the Parent Facilitators Program, uses Title I to implement a ten-week parent training course. Parents learn how to lead parent groups, develop parent/child learning pacts, and promote child outreach activities.

In Louisville, Kentucky and in Little Rock, Arkansas, we learned that Title I funds are used to reduce class size in elementary schools, provide additional help in science and math courses, and provide interdisciplinary teacher planning. Those are only a few examples of how federal efforts combined with state and local efforts will raise achievement standards and ensure that the American workforce in the 21st Century remains the world's best.

These and other witnesses who testified in support of a strong federal role in education represent the views of the public in general, who overwhelmingly support additional federal aid for education. In a "Dollars to the Classroom"[11] hearing, another of the Majority's attempt to undermine the federal role in education backfired. Their own witness, Dr. Barbara Nielsen, Superintendent of Education, State of South Carolina, testified that of the seven percent of funds received from the federal government, "most of it gets to the classroom... and most of it goes for instruction, instructional support, and what we call general operations."

We believe that federal and local partnerships in education must be continued and strengthened. Only then will we assure that all children have equal access and equal opportunity to quality education, regardless of their social and economic status.

IV. The Democratic Agenda

The Crossroads report ignores the major priorities facing public education. The Clinton Administration and Democrats in Congress have set forth a comprehensive agenda to improve public education. The Republican Crossroads Report failed to address these and other high education priorities:

1. **Public Schools Face a $112 billion School Building Crisis.**[12] Democrats have proposed legislation that would help repair crumbling and overcrowd schools through the issuance of zero-interest bonds. Republicans have already voted against this critical initiative.

2. **Class sizes Remain Unacceptably High**. Large class sizes significantly undermine student achievement. Studies confirm that small class sizes promote effective

---

[11] May 8, 1997
[12] In February 1995, a General Accounting Office (GAO) report, *School Facilities: Condition of America's Schools* (GAO/HEHS-95-61), estimated that it would cost about $112 billion in capital improvements to restore America's

teaching and learning. Democrats have proposed a $12 billion initiative over seven years to help local schools provide small classes in the early grades.

3. **Too many Classrooms Lack Competent Teachers.** The key to achieving high academic standards requires small class sizes with teachers who are qualified to teach. Democrats have proposed states implement basic skills testing for new teachers, as a condition for receiving funds for class size reductions. The funds could also be spent on helping teachers improve reading instruction; providing mentors or other support for newly hired teachers; and providing incentives to recruit qualified teachers to high poverty schools. Democrats have also made substantial proposals for enhancing and revamping teacher training programs at institutions of higher education.

4. **Many High Poverty Communities Lack Resources to Renew their Public Schools Alone.** Democrats have proposed comprehensive measures to address the needs of high poverty school districts through the introduction of legislation to create Education Opportunity Zones (H.R. 3813) and fund public school renewal projects. H.R. 3813 is designed to strengthen public schools and help students master the basics where the need is the greatest: in high poverty urban and rural communities where low expectations, too many poorly prepared teachers and wholly inadequate facilities are commonplace. The bill will invest $1.5 billion over 5 years, to raise achievement and share lessons learned with school districts around the country. H.R. 1436, the Public Schools Renewal and Improvement Act, provides assistance to locally-driven public school renewal efforts.

---

multi-billion dollar investment in schools to good overall condition. The GAO report expressed concerns about the ability of schools to provide adequate instructional programs with inadequate buildings and equipment.

5. **Resources for Early Childhood Learning are Substantially Inadequate**.

Research shows that children's experiences in the earliest years are critical to their development and future success. President Clinton has proposed an Early Learning Fund to provide challenge grants to communities to support programs to improve early learning and quality and safe child care for children ages 1-5. The Clinton Administration has also proposed to increase investment in Head Start by $3.4 billion over five years; the plan would also double the number of children served by Early Head Start. Head Start provides early, continuous and comprehensive child development and family support services.

V. Conclusion

It is clear to us that as the Majority stood at the Crossroads on Education, they decided to ignore what the people want and what our children need. They chose a narrow, political, and partisan path, fueled by empty rhetoric while parents, teachers and local schools across the nation are struggling to solve the real problems: crumbling and overcrowded schools, large class sizes, teacher performance, and improving technology in the schools. The Crossroads road-show has come up empty.

Appendix Index

1. Majority to Minority witness ratio

2. List of Federal education programs

3. 10 Department of Education Programs that impact K-12 student performance

4. Title I studies

5. State administrative costs for Formula Grant Programs

APPENDIX 1

HEARING	DEMOCRAT	REPUBLICAN	TOTAL
NAPA	1	10	11
SAN FERNANDO	1	10	11
PHOENIX	2	10	12
WILMINGTON	0	15	15
LAMAR&DELAINE	1	1	2
MILLEDGEVILLE	2	11	13
DC SCHOOLS	1	8	9
NEW YORK	3	12	15
DOLLARS	0	7	7
CINCINNATI	2	9	11
LOUISVILLE	2	9	11
LITTLE ROCK	2	9	11
DRUGPREVENTION	1	3	4
TEACHER TRAIN.	1	4	5
CLEVELAND	2	20	22
MUSKEGON HEIGHTS	1	11	12
DES MOINES	1	13	14
TIMNATH	2	10	12
LEWISBERRY	1	7	8
TOTAL	26	189	215

K-12 Education (142 programs)

U.S. Department of ED

21st Century Community Learning Centers Program (84.287) (ED)

Alaska Native Educational Equity, Support, and Assistance (ED)

Allen J. Ellender Fellowship Program (84.148) (ED)

Arts in Education (ED)

Bilingual Education: Comprehensive School Grants (84.290u) (ED)

Bilingual Education: Comprehensive School Grants (84.291r) (ED)

Bilingual Education: General Research Programs (84.292a) (ED)

Bilingual Education: Graduate Fellowship Program (ED)

Bilingual Education: Program Development and Implementation Grants (84.288s)

Bilingual Education: Program Enhancement Grants (84.289p) (ED)

Bilingual Education; System wide Improvement Grants (84.291r) (ED)

Bilingual Education Teacher and Personnel Program (ED)

Challenge Grants for Technology in Education (84.303) (ED)

Clearinghouse for Individuals with Disabilities (84.030) (ED)

Comprehensive Regional Assistance Centers (84.283) (ED)

Desegregation Assistance, Civil Rights Training, and Advisory Services (84.004) (ED)

Drug-Free Schools and Communities: National Programs (84.184) (ED)

Early Education for Children with Disabilities (ED)

Eisenhower Professional Development: National Activities (ED)

Eisenhower Professional Development State Grants (ED)

ESEA Title I Capital Expenses (84.216) (ED)

ESEA Title I Program for Neglected and Delinquent Children (84.013) (ED)

Even Start: State Educational Agencies (ED)

Foreign Languages Assistance (84.293) (ED)

Funds for the Improvement of Education: Activities (84.215) (ED)

Goals 2000: Parental Assistance Programs (84.310) (ED)

Goals 2000: State and Local Education Systematic Improvement Grants (84.276) (ED)

Helen Keller National Center for Deaf-Blind Youths and Adults (84.128d) (ED)

IDEA Deaf-Blindness Clearinghouse (84.025) (ED)

IDEA Deaf-Blindness Research, Development, Demonstrations (84.025) (ED)

IDEA Deaf-Blindness State Projects (84.025) (ED)

IDEA Early Childhood Demonstrations (ED)

IDEA Early Childhood Experimental (ED)

IDEA Early Childhood Outreach (ED)

IDEA Early Childhood Research (ED)

IDEA Early Childhood Special Projects (ED)

IDEA Early Childhood Tech. Assistance (ED)

IDEA Part B Pre-School Grants (ED)

IDEA Part H Infants and Families (ED)

IDEA Video Described Television (84.026) (ED)

IDEA Recording for the Blind (84.026) (ED)

IDEA Part B Grants to State (84.027) (ED)

IDEA: Regional Resource Centers (84.028) (ED)

IDEA Parent Training (84.029) (ED)

IDEA Personnel Development Grants to IHE's (84.029) (ED)

IDEA Personnel Development Minority Outreach (84.029) (ED)

IDEA Personnel Development Partnerships (84.029) (ED)

IDEA Personnel Development SEA Grants (84.029) (ED)

IDEA Personnel Development Special Projects (84.029) (ED)

IDEA Secondary and Transitional Joint Awards (84.158) (ED)

IDEA Secondary and Transitional Models/Demonstration (84.158) (ED)

IDEA Secondary and Transitional Outreach (84.158) (ED)

IDEA Secondary and Transitional Research (84.158) (ED)

IDEA Secondary and Transitional Services Projects (84.158) (ED)

IDEA SED Demonstrations (84.086) (ED)

IDEA Severe Disabilities Research and Demonstrations (84.086) (ED)

IDEA Severe Disabilities Statewide System (84.086) (ED)

IDEA Technology Applications (84.180) (ED)

Immigrant Education (84.162) (ED)

Impact Aid Basic Support Payments (83.041) (ED)

Impact Aid: Construction (ED)

Impact Aid Disability Payments (84.041) (ED)

Impact Aid Heavily Impacted Districts (84.041) (ED)

Impact Aid Payments for Federal Property (84.041) (ED)

Indian Education: Grants to Local Educational Agencies (84.060) (ED)

Inexpensive Book Distribution Program (ED)

Innovative Education Program Strategies (84.298) (ED)

International Education Exchange (84.304) (ED)

Magnet Schools Assistance (84.165) (ED)

Media and Captioning Services for Individuals with Disabilities (84.026) (ED)

Migrant Education: Basic State Grant Program (84.011) (ED)

Migrant Education: High School Equivalency Program (84.141) (ED)

Minority Teacher Recruitment (84.262) (ED)

National Center for Education Statistics (84.117) (ED)

National Institute on Early Childhood Development and Education (84.307) (ED)

National Institute on the Education of At-Risk Students (84.306) (ED)

National Institute on Educational Governance, Finance, Policy making, and Management (84.308) (ED)

National Institute on Student Achievement, Curriculum, and Assessment (84.305) (ED)

National Vocational Education National Programs/Research (84.051) (ED)

National Writing Project (ED)

Native Hawaiian Community-Based Education Learning Centers (84.296) (ED)

Native Hawaiian Curriculum Development, Teacher Training and Recruitment (84.297) (ED)

Native Hawaiian Family Based Education Centers (84.209) (ED)

Native Hawaiian Gifted and Talented (84.210) (ED)

Native Hawaiian Special Education (84.221) (ED)

OERI: Assessment (ED)

Program Protection and Advocacy of Individual Rights (84.240)

Public Charter Schools (84.282) (ED)

Ready-To-Learn Television (84.295) (ED)

Regional Math and Science Consortia (ED)

Rehabilitation Services: Vocational Rehabilitation Grants to States (84.126) (ED)

Safe and Drug-Free Schools and Communities: State Grants (84.184) (ED)

School-to-Work (84.278) (ED)

Services for Children with Deaf-Blindness (84.025) (ED)

Special Education: Innovation and Development (84.023) (ED)

Special Education: Special Studies for Persons with Disabilities (84.159) (ED)

Technical Support and Professional Development Consortia for Technology (84.302) (ED)

Tech-Prep Education (ED)

Telecommunications Demonstration Project for Mathematics (84.286) (ED)

Title I Grants to Local Education Agencies (84.010) (ED)

Vocational Education: Basic Grants to States (84.048) (ED)

Women's Educational Equity Act Program (84.083) (ED)

U.S. Department of Agriculture

AG. In the Classroom (USDA)

Distance Learning and Medical Link Grants (10.855) (USDA)

Department of Commerce

Earth Resources and Information for Systemic Education (Earthrise) (DOC)

Lockheed Martin Graduate Fellowship Program (DOC)

Operation Pathfinder (DOC)

Practical Hands-On Application to Science Education (DOC)

Corporation for National Service

Learn and Serve America: School and Community Based Programs (94.004)(Corp. Nat'l Serv)

Department of Energy

Albert Einstein Distinguished Educator Fellowship Act/ Fellowship Program (DOE)

Environmental Protection Agency

Environmental Education and Training Program (66.950) (EPA)

U.S. Department of Health and Human Services

Community Schools Program (93.588) (HHS)

Head Start (93.600)

President's Council on Physical Fitness and Sports (93.289) (HHS)

Research Infrastructure: Science Education Partnership Award (93.389) (HHS)

Research Infrastructure: NCRR Minority Initiative Program: K-12 Teachers and High School Students (93.389) (HHS)

U.S. Department of Interior

Area/Agency Technical Support (DOI)

Bureau of Indian Affairs: Tribal Departments of Education (DOI)

Education (Tribal Design) (DOI)

Federal Indian Schools: Administrative Cost Grants (DOI)

Federal Indian Schools: Early Childhood Education (DOI)

Federal Indian Schools: Indian School Equalization Program (DOI)

Indian Education: Assistance to Schools (15.130) (DOI)

Indian School Equalization (ISEP) Program Adjustments (DOI)

Institutional Handicapped (DOI)

ISEP. Student Transportation BIA (DOI)

U.S. Department of Justice

Desegregation of Public Schools (16.100) (DOJ)

U.S. Department of Transportation

Aviation Education (DOT)

U.S. Department of Treasury
Gang Resistance Education and Training (GREAT) (Treasury)

U.S. Institute of Peace
Education and Training Program (National Peace Essay Contest) (U.S. Inst. Of Peace)
Education and Training Program (Summer Institute for Secondary School Teachers (U.S. Inst. Of Peace)

National Science Foundation
Education and Human Resources (47.076) (NSF)
Teacher Preparation and Enhancement (47.066) (NSF)

United States Information Agency
Educational Exchange - Fulbright Teacher Program (USIA)
International Educational Exchange: Congress-Bundestag Youth Exchange Program (USIA)
International Educational Exchange: German American Partnership Program (USIA)
International Educational Exchange: NIS Secondary School Initiative (USIA)

National Aeronautics and Space Administration
Aerospace Education Services Program (Spacemobile) (43.001) (NASA)
NASA Education Program, Education Technology (NASA)
NASA Education Program, Student Programs, Elementary and Secondary (NASA)
NASA Education Program, Teacher/Faculty Programs, El&Sec (NASA)
Support for Systemic Change/Innovative Reform Initiatives (NASA)

Postsecondary and Adult Education (139 programs)

U.S. Department of Education
Adult Education: State Grant Program (ED)
American Overseas Research Centers (84.274) (ED)
Business and International Education Projects (84.153) (ED)
Byrd Honors Scholarships (84.185) (ED)
Calvin Coolidge Memorial Foundation (one-time appropriation) (ED)
Centers for International Business Education (84.220) (ED)
Claiborne Pell Institute for International Relations and Public Policy (One-time appropriation) (ED)
The Edmund Muskie Foundation (One-time appropriation)
Federal Pell Grant Program (84.063) (ED)
Federal Perkins Loans: capitol contributions (84.037) (ED)
Federal Supplemental Educational Opportunity Grants (84.007) (ED)

Federal Work-Study Program (84.033) (ED)

FFEL Consolidation Loans (84.032) (ED)

FFEL: Plus Loans (84.032) (ED)

FFEL Stafford Subsidized Loans (84.032) (ED)

FFEL Unsubsidized Stafford Loans (84.032) (ED)

Foreign Language and Area Studies Fellowship (84.015) (ED)

Fund for the Improvement of Postsecondary Education: Comprehensive Program (84.116) (ED)

Fund for the Improvement of Postsecondary Education: Special Focus Program (84.116) (ED)

Gallaudet University: University Programs (84.994K) (ED)

George Bush Fellowship Program (One-time Appropriation) (ED)

Graduate Assistance in Areas of National Need (84.200) (ED)

HEA: College Assistance Migrant Program (84.149) (ED)

HEA Strengthening Institutions (84.031A) (ED)

Higher Education: TRIO Staff Training Program (84.103) (ED)

Historically Black College and University Capital Financing Program (ED)

Howard University, Academic Program (ED)

Institute for International Public Policy (ED)

International: Overseas Seminars Abroad - Bilateral Projects (84.018) (ED)

International Research and Studies Projects (84.017) (ED)

Javits Fellowships (84.170) (ED)

Language Resource Centers (84.229) (ED)

Literacy Programs for Prisoners (84.255) (ED)

Mary McLeod Bethune Memorial Fine Arts Center (ED)

McNair Post-Baccalaureate Achievement (84.217) (ED)

Minority Science Improvement (84.120) (ED)

National Institute for Literacy (84.257) (ED)

National Institute of Postsecondary Education, Libraries, and Lifelong Learning (84.309) (ED)

National Early Intervention Scholarships and Partnerships (ED)

National Resource Centers and Fellowships Program for Language and Area or Language and Interernational Studies (84.015) (ED)

National Technical Institute of the Deaf (ED)

Native Hawaiian Higher Education Program (84.316) (ED)

NIDRR Dissemination and Utilization (84.133) (ED)

NIDRR: Field-Initiated Research (ED)

NIDRR: Rehabilitation And Training Centers (ED)

NIDRR: Research and Demonstrations (ED)

NIDRR: Spinal Cord Injury Centers (ED)

OPE: Interest Subsidy Grants, OPE (ED)

Perkins Loan Cancellations (84.037) (ED)

Postsecondary Education Programs for Persons with Disabilities (84.078) (ED)

Projects with Industry (84.234) (ED)

Rehabilitation Engineering Research Centers (ED)

Rehabilitation Services: Client Assistance Programs (84.161) (ED)

Rehabilitation Services: Independent Living Services for Older Individuals who are Blind (84.177) (ED)

Rehabilitation Short-Term Training (84.246) (ED)

Rehabilitative Training: Continuing Education (84.264) (ED)

Rehabilitation Training: General Training (84.275) (ED)

Rehabilitation Training: State Vocational Rehabilitation Unit In-Service Training (ED)

Special Projects and Demonstrations for Providing Vocational Rehabilitation Services to Individuals with Severe Disabilities (84.235) (ED)

State Grants for Assistive Technology (84.224) (ED)

State Student Incentives Grants (84.069) (ED)

Strengthening HBCUs (84.031B) (ED)

Strengthening Hispanic Serving Institutions (84.031A) (ED)

Supported Employment Services for Individuals with Severe Disabilities (84.187) (ED)

Training Interpreters for Individuals who are Deaf and Individuals who are Deaf-Blind (84.160) (ED)

TRIO: Educational Opportunity Centers (84.066) (ED)

TRIO: Student Support Services (84.042) (ED)

TRIO: Talent Search (84.044) (ED)

TRIO: Upward Bound (84.047) (ED)

Undergraduate International Studies and Foreign Language Programs (84.016) (ED)

Urban Community Service (84.252) (ED)

Vocational Education: Tribally Controlled Postsecondary Institutions (ED)

Vocational Rehabilitation to States (ED)

William D. Ford Direct Consolidated Loans (84.268) (ED)

William D. Ford Direct Subsidized Stafford Loans (84.268) (ED)

William D. Ford Direct Unsubsidized Stafford Loans (84.268) (ED)

William D. Ford PLUS Loans (ED)

U.S. Department of Agriculture

1890 Institution Capacity Building Grants (CFDA 10.216) (USDA)

Food and Agricultural Sciences National Needs Graduate Fellowship Grants (CFDA 10.510) (USDA)

Higher Education Challenge Grants (10.217) (USDA)

Higher Education Multicultural Scholars Program (10.220) (USDA)

Tribal Colleges Endowment Funds (10.222) (USDA)

U.S. Department of Commerce
Cooperative Science and Education Program (DOC)

Environmental Research Laboratories Cooperative Institutes (11.432) (DOC)

National Research Council Postdoctoral Research Associateships (DOC)

NOAA Earth Systems Science Program (DOC)

Sea Grant Support (11.417), (DOC)

Corporation for National Service
Learn and Serve America: Higher Education (94.005)

U.S. Department of Defense
Armed Forces Health Professions Scholarship Program (DOD)

Mathematical Sciences Grants Program (12.901), National Security Agency (DOD)

Military Service Academies (DOD)

Montgomery GI Bill, Selected Reserve Educational Assistance Program (DOD)

ROTC (DOD)

Uniformed Services (DOD)

U.S. Department of Energy
Academic Partnerships (CFDA 81.102) (DOE)

Minority Educational Institution Assistance (81.094) (DOE)

Environmental Protection Agency
Graduate Environmental Education Grants or Star Graduate Environmental Education Fellowships (EPA)

Independent Scholarships/Fellowships not related to an Agency
Barry Goldwater Scholarship Program

Harry S. Truman Scholarship Foundation

James Madison Memorial Fellowship Program

U.S. Department of Health and Human Services
Clinical Research Loan Repayment Program for Individuals from Disadvantaged Backgrounds (93.220) (HHS)

Demonstration Grants to States for Community Scholarships (93.931) (HHS)

Developmental Disabilities University Affiliated Programs (93.632), (HHS)

Grants for State Loan Repayment (93.165) (HHS)

National Health Service Corps Scholarship Program (93.288)

Senior International Fellowships (93.989) (HHS)

Special Minority Initiatives (93.960) (HHS)

Undergraduate Scholarship Program for Individuals from Disadvantaged Backgrounds (93.187) (HHS)

U.S. Department of Housing and Urban Development
Community Development Work-Study Program (14.512) (HUD)

U.S. Department of Interior

Adult Education

Federal Postsecondary Schools for Indians (DOI)

Scholarships, IPA, (15.114) (DOI)

Special Higher Education Scholarships (DOI)

Tribally Controlled Community Colleges—Land & Grant Status (DOI)

United Tribes Technical College (DOI)

U.S. Department of Justice

Criminal Justice Research and Development Graduate Research Fellowships (16.562) (DOJ)

Law Enforcement Scholarships (No CFDA)

Police Corps Scholarships (DOJ)

National Aeronautics and Space Administration

NASA Education Program, Student Programs, Postsecondary Programs (NASA)

NASA Education Program, Teacher/Faculty Programs, Higher Education (NASA)

NASA Minority University Research and Education Division: Historically Black Colleges and Universities (NASA)

NASA Minority University Research and Education Division: Other Minority Universities (NASA)

Support for Systemic Change/National Space Grant College and Fellowship Program (NASA)

National Endowment for the Humanities

Promotion of the Humanities - Education Development and Demonstration (45.162) (NEH)

National Science Foundation

Graduate Fellowships (47.009) (NSF)

Human Resource Development (47.069) (Small part is pre-college) (NSF)

Science and Technology Centers (small K-12 outreach component) (NSF)

Undergraduate Science, Engineering, and Mathematics Education (47.071) (NSF)

Social Security Administration

Vocational Rehabilitation Services (Social Security Administration)

U.S. Department of Transportation
Airway Science (20.107), (DOT)

Student Training and Education Program (20.902) (DOT)

U.S. Merchant Marine Academy (20.807) (DOT)

University Transportation Centers Programs (20.701), (DOT)

United States Agency for International Development
American Schools and Hospitals Abroad (AID)

United States Information Agency
Educational Exchange: Fulbright Student Program (82.001) (USIA)

Educational Exchange: University Lecturers and Research Scholars (82.002) (USIA)

International Educational Exchange: Special Academic Exchanges (USIA)

U.S. Department of Veterans' Affairs
All-Volunteer Force Educational Assistance (64.124) (DVA)

Survivors and Dependents Educational Assistance (64.117) (DVA)

Arts/Museums/Historic Preservation (27 programs)

Independent
Institute of Museum Services (45.301)

U.S. Department of Interior
Historic American Buildings Survey/Historic American Engineering Record (15.410), (DOI)

Historic American Buildings Survey/Historic American Engineering Record (15.909) (DOI)

National Archives
Multimedia and Publications Distribution (89.002) (NArch)

National Archives and Records Administration (NArch)

National Historical Publications and Records Grants (89.003) (NArch)

National Endowment for the Arts
Arts and Artifacts Indemnity (45.201) (NEA)

Promotion of the Arts - Grants to Organizations and Individuals (45.024) (NEA)

Promotion of the Arts - Leadership Initiatives (45.026) (NEA)

Promotion of the Arts - Partnership Agreement (45.025) (NEA)

National Endowment for the Humanities
Promotion of the Humanities: Challenge Grants (45.130) (NEH)

Promotion of the Humanities - Division of Preservation and Access (45.149) (NEH)

National Gallery of Art
National Gallery of Art Extension Service

The Smithsonian Institution

Anacostia Museum (Smithsonian)

Center of Museum Studies (Smithsonian)

Cooper-Hewitt Museum (Smithsonian)

Hirshorn Museum and Sculpture Garden (Smithsonian)

National Air and Space Museum (Smithsonian)

National Museum of American Art (Smithsonian)

National Museum of American History (Smithsonian)

National Museum of the American Indian (Smithsonian)

National Museum of Natural History (Smithsonian)

National Science Resources Center (Smithsonian)

National Zoological Park (Smithsonian)

Office of Elem.&Second. Ed. (Smithsonian)

Smithsonian Astrophysical Observatory (Smithsonian)

Smithsonian Tropical Research Institute (Smithsonian)

Services to Individuals (26 programs)

Department of Education

Centers for Independent Living (84.132) (ED)

Independent Living: State Grants (84.169) (ED)

U.S. Department of Health and Human Services

Adolescent Health Centers for American Indians/Alaska Natives (93.158), (HHS)

Block Grants for Community Mental Health Services (93.958), (HHS)

Child Abuse Prevention and Treatment Act: Community Based Family Resource and Support (93.590) (HHS)

Child Abuse Prevention and Treatment Act: Federal Discretionary Activities (93.607) (HHS)

Child Abuse Prevention and Treatment Act: Grants to Improve Investigation and Prosecution (HHS)

Child Abuse Prevention and Treatment Act: State Grants for Prevention and Treatment (93.669) (HHS)

Child Care and Development Block Grant (93.575), (HHS)

Comprehensive Residential Drug Prevention and Treatment Projects for Substance-Using Women and Their Children (93.937), (HHS)

Grants to States for Planning and Development of Dependent Care Programs (93.673), (HHS)

Independent Living (93.674) (HHS)

Linking Community-Based Primary Care, Substance Abuse, HIV/AIDS, and Mental Health Treatment Services (93.109), (HHS)

Mental Health Disaster Assistance and Emergency Mental Health (93.982),(HHS)

Preventive Health Services: Sexually Transmitted Diseases Control Grants (93.977) (HHS)

Projects for Assistance in Transition from Homelessness (PATH) (93.982), (HHS)

Refugee and Entrant Assistance: Discretionary Grants (93.576), (HHS)

Refugee and Entrant Assistance: State Administered Programs (93.566), (HHS)

Refugee Assistance: Voluntary Agency Programs. (CFDA 93.567), (HHS)

Residents of Public Housing Primary Care Program (93.927) (HHS)

Runaway and Homeless Youth (93.623) (HHS)

Special Programs for the Aging--Title III Part B--Grants for Supportive Services and Senior Centers (93.044) (HHS)

Urban Indian Health Services (93.193) (HHS)

U.S. Department of Justice

Child Abuse Prevention and Treatment Act: Missing Children (16.543) (DOJ)

Child Abuse Prevention and Treatment Act: Children's Advocacy Centers (16.547) (DOJ)

Juvenile Justice and Delinquency Prevention: Allocation to States (16.540) (DOJ)

Community Development/Community Service/Construction (16 programs)

U.S. Department of Agriculture

Community Facilities Loans (10.766) (USDA)

Rural Technology Development Grants (10.771) (USDA)

Schools and Roads - Grants to Counties (10.666), (USDA)

Schools and Roads - Grants to States (10.665), (USDA)

Appalachian Regional Commission

Appalachian Local Access Roads (23.008) (ARC)

U.S. Department of Commerce

Congressionally Identified Construction Projects (11.469) (DOC)

Public Telecommunications Facilities Program (11.550) (DOC)

Corporation for National Service

AmeriCorps: Grants Programs (Corp. Nat'l Serv)

Foster Grandparent Program. (94.011) (Corp. Nat'l Serv)

National Civilian Community Corps (Corp. Nat'l Serv)

Retired Senior Volunteer Program (94.002) (Corp. Nat'l Serv)

Volunteers In Service To America (94.013) (Corp. Nat'l Serv)

U.S. Department of Defense

Protection of Essential Highways, Highway Bridge Approaches, and Public Works (12.105) (DOD)

U.S. Department of Energy

Regional Biomass Energy Programs (81.079) (DOE)

U.S. Department of Interior

Facilities Operation and Maintenance (DOI)

United Sioux Tribes Development Corporation (DOI)

Health Professionals Education and Training (58 programs)

U.S. Department of Health and Human Services

Advanced Nurse Education (93.299), (HHS)

Alcohol National Research Service Awards for Research Training (93.272) (HHS)

Allied Health Project Grants, National Institutes of Health (HHS)

Area Health Education Centers (93.824) (HHS)

Cancer Research Manpower (93.398) (HHS)

Clinical Training Grant for Faculty Development in Alcohol and Other Drug Abuses (93.274), (HHS)

Contraception and Infertility Loan Repayment Plan (93.209), (HHS)

Disadvantaged Health Professions Faculty Loan Repayment and Fellowship Program (93.923), (HHS)

Drug Abuse National Research Awards for Research Training (93.278) (HHS)

Educating Health Professionals Regarding Environmentally Hazardous Substances, (HHS)

Financial Assistance for Disadvantaged Health Professions Students (93.139) (HHS)

Grants for Establishment of Departments of Family Medicine (93.984), (HHS)

Grants for Faculty Development in Family Medicine (93.895), (HHS)

Grants for Faculty Development in General Internal Medicine and/or General Pediatrics (93.900), (HHS)

Grants for Faculty Training Projects in Geriatric Medicine and Dentistry, (HHS)

Grants for Geriatric Education Centers (93.969), (HHS)

Grants for Graduate Training in Family Medicine (93.379), (HHS)

Grants for Nurse Anesthetist Faculty Fellowships (93.907),(HHS)

Grants for Physician Assistant Training Program, (HHS)

Grants for Podiatric Primary Care Residency Training (93.181) (HHS)

Grants for Predoctoral Training in Family Medicine (93.896), (HHS)

Grants for Preventive Medicine and Dental Public Health (93.117), (HHS)

Grants for Residency Training in General Internal Medicine and/or General Pediatrics (93.884), (HHS)

Health Administration Traineeships and Special Projects Programs (93.962), (HHS)

Health Careers Opportunity Program (93.822) (HHS)

Health Education Assistance Loans (93.108) (HHS)

Health Education and Training Centers (93.189), (HHS)

Health Professions Pregraduate Scholarships Programs for Indians (93.970), (HHS)

Health Professions Preparatory Scholarship Program for Indians (93.971) (HHS)

Health Professions Recruitment Program for Indians (93.970) (HHS)

Health Professions Scholarship Program (93.972) (HHS)

Health Professions Student Loans, Including Primary Care Loans/Loans for Disadvantaged Students (93.342) (HHS)

Indian Health Service Educational Loan Repayment (93.164) (HHS)

Interdisciplinary Training for Health Care for Rural Areas (93.192) (HHS)

Matching Grants for Health Professions Scholarships to Indian Tribes (93.219) (HHS)

Mental Health National Research Service Awards for Research Training (93.282) (HHS)

National AIDS Education and Training Centers (93.145), (HHS)

National Institutes of Health Acquired Immunodeficiency Syndrome Research Loan Repayment Program (93.936),(HHS)

National Research Services Awards, National Institutes of Health (HHS)

Nurse Anesthetist Education Programs (93.916), (HHS)

Nurse Anesthetist Traineeship (93.124), (HHS)

Nursing Education Loan Repayment Program for Registered Nurses Entering Employment at Eligible Health Facilities (93.908), (HHS)

Nursing Education Opportunities for Individuals from Disadvantaged Backgrounds (93.178), (HHS)

Nurse Practitioner and Nurse-Midwifery Education Programs (93.298), (HHS)

Nurse Training Improvement Special Projects (93.359) (HHS)

Nursing Student Loans (93.364) (HHS)

Occupational Safety and Health: Training Grants (93.263), (HHS)

Pilot Clinical Pharmacology Training (93.948), Food and Drug Administration (HHS)

Professional Nurse Traineeships (93.358), (HHS)

Programs of Excellence in Health Professions Education for Minorities (93.157), (HHS)

Public Health Traineeships (93.964) (HHS)

Residency Training and Advanced Education in the General Practice of Dentistry (93.897), Health Resources and Services Administration (HHS)

Resource and Manpower Development in the Environmental Health Sciences (93.894), (HHS)

Rural Health Medical Education Demonstration Projects (93.906), (HHS)

Scholarships for Health Professions Students for Disadvantaged Backgrounds (93.925)

Scholarships for Students of Exceptional Financial Need (93.820) (HHS)

Special Project Grants to Schools of Public Health (93.188) (HHS)

Tuberculosis Demonstration, Research, Public and Professional Education (93.947), (HHS)

Nutrition (11 programs)

U.S. Department of Agriculture

Child and Adult Care Food Program (10.558) (USDA)

Food Distribution (10.550) (USDA)

Food Stamps, (10.551) (USDA)

Interdisciplinary Training for Health Care for Rural Areas (93.192),(HHS)

National School Lunch Program (10.555) (USDA)

Family Resource Centers, Administration for Children and Families (HHS)

HIV/AIDS Prevention and Health Communication Programs (HHS)

HIV Prevention Activities: Non-Governmental Organization Based (93.939), (HHS)

Immunization Research, Demonstration, Public Information, and Education: Training and Clinical Skills Improvement Projects (93.185) (HHS)

Mental Retardation: President's Committee on Mental Retardation (93.613) (HHS)

Minority AIDS and Related Risk Factors Education/Prevention Grants (93.939) (HHS)

Minority Community-Based HIV Prevention Projects (93.939)

Minority and Other Community-Based Human Immunodeficiency Virus Prevention Projects (93.939) (HHS)

National/Regional Minority Organization HIV/STD, and TB Prevention (93.939) (HHS)

Preventive Health and Health Services Block Grant (93.991), (HHS)

Preventive Health Services: Sexually Transmitted Diseases Research, Demonstrations, and Public Information and Education Grants (93.978), (HHS)

Rape Prevention and Education (No CFDA) "at least 25% of the monies are devoted to education programs targeted for middle, junior high, and high school." (HHS)

Youth Education and Domestic Violence (HHS)

U.S. Department of Housing and Urban Development

Fair Housing Initiatives Program Education and Outreach Initiative (14.409) (HUD)

U.S. Department of Interior

Clean Vessel Act (15.616), U.S. Fish and Wildlife Service (DOI)

U.S. Department of Justice

Crime Prevention - Ounce of Prevention Grants (95.002) (DOJ)

Public Education on Drug Abuse: Information (16.005) (DOJ)

Library of Congress

Books for the Blind and Physically Handicapped (42.001) (LOC)

Distribution of Library of Congress Cataloging (42.003) (LOC)

Library of Congress Constituent and Collection Services (42.006) (LOC)

Library of Congress Publications (42.005) (LOC)

Reference Services in Science and Technology (42.007) (LOC)

National Aeronautics and Space Administration

Technology Transfer (43.002) (NASA)

National Endowment for the Humanities

Promotion of the Humanities - Federal State Partnership (45.129) (NEH)

Promotion of the Humanities - Public Programs (45.164) (NEH)

Nuclear Regulatory Commission

Enhance Technology Transfer and Dissemination of Nuclear Process and Safety Information (77.003) (NRC)

Financial Assistance for Nuclear Regulatory Commission (77.005) (NRC)

Nutrition Education and Training Program (10.564) (USDA)

School Breakfast Program (10.553) (USDA)

Special Milk Program for Children (10.556) (USDA)

Special Supplemental Food Program for Women, Infants, and Children (10.557) (USDA)

State Administrative Expenses for Child Nutrition (10.560), (USDA)

Summer Food Service Program for Children (10.559), (USDA)

Public Information/Community Outreach (47 programs)

U.S. Department of Education

ERIC Clearinghouse (84.117) (ED)

American Printing House for the Blind (84.998V) (ED)

U.S. Department of Agriculture

Agricultural Telecommunications Program (10.501) (USDA)

National Agricultural Library (10.700) (USDA)

U.S. Department of Commerce

National Marine Sanctuary Program (11.429) (DOC)

Telecommunications and Information Infrastructure Assistance Program (11.552) (DOC)

U.S. Department of Energy

State Energy Conservation Program (DOE)

Environmental Protection Agency

Environmental Education Grants (66.951) (EPA)

Government Printing Office

Depository Libraries for Government Publications (40.001) (GPO)

Government Publications Sales and Distribution (40.002) (GPO)

U.S. Department of Health and Human Services

Acquired Immunodeficiency Syndrome (AIDS) Activity (CFDA 93.118), (HHS)

Adolescent Family Life: Demonstration Projects (93.995), (HHS)

Bilingual/Bicultural Service Demonstration Grant Program (93.105) (HHS)

Centers for Agricultural Research, Education and Disease and Injury Prevention and Occupational Disease and Musculoskeletal Disorders (93.956) (HHS)

Childhood Lead Poisoning Prevention Projects: State and Community-Based Childhood Lead Poisoning Prevention and Surveillance of Blood Lead Levels in Children (93.197) (HHS)

Cooperative Agreements to Support Comprehensive School Health Programs to Prevent the Spread of HIV... (93.938) (HHS)

Educational Training to Reduce Sexual Abuse of Runaway, Homeless, and Street Youth (HHS)

Family and Community Violence Prevention Program (93.910), (HHS)

Family Planning: Services (93.217) (HHS)

U.S. Department of Transportation
Boating Safety Financial Assistance (CFDA 20.005), (DOT)

Specialized Research (71 programs)

U.S. Department of Agriculture
Animal Health and Disease Research (CFDA 10.207) (USDA)

ARS Research Apprentice Program

International Agricultural Research Program (CFDA 10.961) (USDA)

Technical Agricultural Assistance (10.960) (USDA)

U.S. Department of Commerce
Coastal Zone Management Estuarine Research Reserves (11.420) (DOC)

U.S. Department of Defense
Air Force Defense Research Sciences Program (12.800) (DOD)

Military Medical Research and Development (12.420) (DOD)

U.S. Department of Energy
Basic Energy Sciences: University and Science Education (CFDA 81.049) (DOE)

Minority Educational Institution Research Travel Fund (CFDA 81.083), (DOE)

University Coal Research (CFDA 81.057) (DOE)

University Reactor Sharing and Fuel Assistance (CFDA 12.105) (DOE)

Waste Management Education Research Consortium (DOE)

U.S. Department of Health and Human Services
Academic Research Enhancement Award, (HHS)

Adolescent Family Life: Research Grants (93.111) (HHS)

Aging Research (93.866) (HHS)

Allergy, Immunology and Transplantation Research (93.855) (HHS)

Arthritis, Musculo-Skeletal and Skin Diseases Research (93.846) (HHS)

Biological Basis Research in the Neurosciences (93.854) (HHS)

Biological Response to Environmental Health Hazards (93.113), (HHS)

Biomedical Technology: Research Manpower Development (93.371), (HHS)

Blood Diseases and Resources Research (93.839) (HHS)

Cell Biology and Biophysics Research (93.821), (HHS)

Center for Medical Rehabilitation Research (93.929), (HHS)

Clinical Research Related to Neurological Disorders (93.853) (HHS)

Clinical Research: Research Career Development (93.333) (HHS)

Community Services Block Grant Discretionary Awards (93.573) (HHS)

Comparative Medicine Research Manpower Development Program (CFDA 93.306), (HHS)

Diabetes, Endocrinology and Metabolism Research (CFDA 93.847), (HHS)

Digestive Diseases and Nutrition Research (CFDA 93.848), (HHS)

Drug Abuse Research Programs (93.279) (HHS)

Family Planning: Service Delivery Improvement Research Grants, (HHS)

Genetics and Developmental Biology Research (93.862) (HHS)

Heart and Vascular Diseases Research (CFDA 93.837), (HHS)

Human Genome Research (93.172) (HHS)

International Cooperative Biodiversity Groups Program (93.168), (HHS)

Intramural Research Training Award, National Institutes of Health (HHS)

Kidney Diseases, Urology and Hematology Research (93.849) (HHS)

Lung Diseases Research (93.383) (HHS)

Mental Health Research Career/Scientist Development Awards, (93.281) (HHS)

Microbiology and Infectious Diseases Research (93.856) (HHS)

Minority Access to Research Career, National Institutes of Health (93.880) (HHS)

Minority Biomedical Research Support, (93.375) National Institutes of Health (HHS)

Minority International Research Training Grant in the Biomedical and Behavioral Sciences, (HHS)

NIEHS Superfund Hazardous Substances: Basic Research and Education (CFDA 93.143), (HHS)

Nursing Research, National Institutes of Health (HHS)

Oral Diseases and Disorders Research (93.121) (HHS)

Pharmacology, Physiology, and Biological Chemistry (93.859) (HHS)

Population Research (93.864) (HHS)

Research and Demonstration Projects for Indian Health (CFDA 93.933), (HHS)

Research for Mothers and Children, (HHS)

Research Related to Deafness and Communication Disorders (93.173) (HHS)

Research and Training in Alternative Medicine (93.213) (HHS)

Vision Research (93.867) (HHS)

U.S. Department of Justice

Juvenile Justice and Delinquency Prevention: Special Emphasis (CFDA 16.541) (DOJ)

U.S. Department of Labor

Employment Services and Job Training: Pilot and Demonstration Programs (CFDA 17.249), (DOL)

Employment and Training Research and Development Projects (CFDA 17.248) (DOL)

National Aeronautics and Space Agency

Support for Systemic Change/Experimental Program to Stimulate Competitive Research (NASA)

National Endowment for the Humanities

Promotion of the Humanities - Research (45.161) (NEH)

Promotion of the Humanities - Fellowship and Stipends (45.160) (NEH)

National Science Foundation

Biological Sciences (CFDA 47.074) (NSF)

Computer and Information Science and Engineering (47.070) (NSF)

Materials Development, Research, and Informal Science Education (47.067) (NSF)

Mathematical and Physical Sciences (CFDA 47.049) (NSF)

Research, Evaluation, and Communication (47.066) (NSF)

Social, Behavioral, and Economic Sciences (CFDA 47.075) (NSF)

U.S. Institute of Peace

International Peace and Conflict Management: Research and Management: Research and Education (91.001) (U.S. Inst. Of Peace)

U.S. Department of Transportation

Air Transportation Centers of Excellence (CFDA 20.109), (DOT)

Aviation Research Grants (CFDA 20.108), (DOT)

University Research Institutes Program (CFDA 20.702), (DOT)

United States Information Agency

International Peace and Conflict Management Articles and Manuscripts (CFDA 91.002) (USIA, NIP)

International Peace and Conflict Management: Research and Education (USIA, NIP)

Employment or Job-Related Training and Technical Assistance (68 programs)

U.S. Department of Agriculture

Small Farmer Outreach Training or Technical Assistance Program (CFDA 10.433) (USDA)

Youth Forest Camps (USDA)

U.S. Department of Commerce

Census Customer Services: Reimbursable Training Workshops (11.002) (DOC)

Cooperative Program for Operational Meteorology, Education and Training (DOC)

Meteorologic and Hydrologic Modernization Development (CFDA 11.467) (DOC)

National Economic Accounting and Training Program for Foreign Nationals (No CFDA) (DOC)

Corporation for National Service

Training and Technical Assistance (CFDA 94.009) (Corp. Nat'l Serv)

U.S. Department of Energy

Science Teacher Workshop Program - Health Physics Society (DOE)

University: Laboratory Cooperative Program (CFDA 81.004) (DOE)

Environmental Protection Agency

Air Pollution Control Manpower Training (CFDA 66.003) (EPA)

Federal Emergency Management Agency

Emergency Management Institute (EMI): Bruce Marshall Emergency management assistance, State and Local Assistance (83.534) (FEMA)

Emergency Management Institute (EMI) Resident Educational Program (83.530) (FEMA)

Emergency Management Institute: Training Assistance (CFDA 83.527) (FEMA)

U.S. Department of Health and Human Services

Child Welfare Services Training Grants (CFDA 93.648), (HHS)

Community Services Block Grant (93.570) (HHS)

Family Planning: Personnel Training, (HHS)

Grants to Community Organizations for Training Personnel in field of aging: technical assistance to agencies responsible for older... (93.048) (HHS)

Improving the Capability of Indian Tribal Governments to Regulate Environmental Quality (CCFDA 93.581), (HHS)

Medical Library Assistance, (93.879) (HHS)

Minority Community Health Coalition Demonstration (93.137) (HHS)

NIEHS Hazardous Waste Worker Health and Safety Training (CFDA 93.142), (HHS)

Technical and Non-Financial Assistance to Community and Migrant Health Centers (CFDA 93.129), (HHS)

U.S. Department of Housing and Urban Development

Public Housing Youth Apprenticeship Program (HUD)

Resident Management Technical Assistance Grants/Tenant Opportunity Program (No CFDA)) (HUD)

State CDBG Technical Assistance (CDTA) set-aside (HUD)

Youth Build Program (14.243) (HUD)

U.S. Department of Interior

Education Program Management (DOI)

Indian Employment Assistance (15.108), (DOI)

Ironworker Training Program (CFDA 15.146), (DOI)

Solo Parent Program (DOI)

U.S. Department of Justice

CAPTA: Technical Assistance to Improve Prosecution 16.547 (DOJ)

Citizen Education and Training (16.400) (DOJ)

Corrections: Technical Assistance/Clearinghouse (CFDA 16.603), (DOJ)

Corrections: Training and Staff Development (CFDA 16.601), (DOJ)

Criminal Justice Discretionary Grant Program (16.574) (DOJ)

Law Enforcement Assistance: FBI Advanced Police Training (CFDA 16.300), (DOJ)

Law Enforcement Assistance: Narcotics and Dangerous Drugs Training (CFDA 16.004), (DOJJ)

National Institute for Juvenile Justice and Delinquency Prevention (CFDA 16.542) (DOJ)

Title V: Delinquency Prevention Program (CFDA 16.548) (DOJ)

U.S. Department of Labor

Apprenticeship Training (17.201) Labor, Employment and Training Administration (DOL)

Disabled Veterans Outreach Programs (17.801) (DOL)

Employment and Training Assistance - Dislocated Workers (17.246), (DOL)

Job Corps (DOL)

Job Training Partnership Act (17.250), (DOL)

Local Veterans Employment Representative Program (17.804) (DOL)

Migrant and Seasonal Farmworkers (17.247), (DOL)

Mine Health and Safety Education and Training (CFDA 17.602), (DOL)

National Skills Standards Board (DOL)

Native American Employment and Training Programs (17.251),(DOL)

Occupational Safety and Health: Training and Education (CFDA 17.502), (DOL)

Senior Community Service Employment Program (17.235), (DOL)

Trade Adjustment Assistance: Workers (17.245), (DOL)

Veterans' Employment Program (17.802), (DOL)

National Endowment for the Humanities

Promotion of the Humanities - Seminars and Institutes (45.163) (NEH)

National Science Foundation

Engineering Grants (47.041) (NSF)

Nuclear Regulatory Commission

Radiation Control: Training Assistance and Advisory Counseling (CFDA 77.001) (NRC)

Small Business Administration

Small Business Development Centers (59.037) (SBA)

Veterans Entrepreneurial Training and Counseling (CFDA 59.044) (SBA)

U.S. Department of Transportation

Coast Guard Reserve Training (No CFDA, No description) (DOT)

Entrepreneurial Training and Technical Assistance: Hispanic Serving Institutions (20.906) (DOT)

Entrepreneurial Training and Technical Assistance: HBCUs (20.907) (DOT)

Highway Training and Education (20.215) (DOT)

Human Resource Programs (CFDA 20.511), (DOT)

Interagency Hazardous Materials Public Sector Training and Planning Grants (CFDA 20.703), (DOT)

State Marine Schools (20.806)(DOT)

Supplementary Training (CFDA 20.810) (DOT)

U.S. Department of Veterans Affairs

Vocational and Educational Counseling for Service- members and Veterans (64.125), (DVA)

Vocational Rehabilitation for Disabled Veterans (CFDA 64.116) (DVA)

Unfunded and Misidentified Items (183 programs)

(* designates programs that the committee acknowledges are either unfunded or deauthorized, citation is in parentheses)

U.S. Department of Education—Unfunded

Alaska and Native Hawaiian Cultural Arts Development Consortia for Technology (84.300)

Bilingual Education: Career Ladder Program

Bilingual Education: National Professional Development Institutes

Bilingual Education Training for all Teachers Program

Bilingual Vocational Instructional Materials, Methods, and Techniques (84.100)

Civics Education: Instruction in Civics, Government and the Law (84.123)

* Class Size Demonstration Grant (K-12, p 11)

College Housing and Academic Facilities Loans (84.142)

* Community Education Employment Centers (p.4)

* Community Schools Partnerships (K-12, p11)

Consolidated Overseas American-Sponsored Schools Assistance Program

Construction, Reconstruction, and Renovation of Academic Facilities (84.172)

Cooperative Education (84.055)

* Delugo and Territorial Education Improvement Program (K-12, p8)

Demonstration Grants for Critical Language/Area Studies

Demonstration and Innovation Projects of National Significance in Assistive Technology for Individuals with Disabilities (84.231)

Douglas Teacher Scholarships (84.176)

* Early Childhood Education Training (ProDev, p3)

* Education Finance Incentive Program (K-12, p 8)

Eisenhower Leadership Program (84.261)

Endowment Challenge Grants (84.031C)

ESEA Title I Migrant Program -- coordination grants (84.144)

ESEA Title I State School Improvement Grants (84.218)

* Extended Time for Learning and Longer School Year (K-12, p7)

Family and Community Endeavor Schools Grant Program (84.285)

Foreign Languages Assistance: Incentive Grants (84.294)

* Foreign Periodicals (Post Sec, p 30)

* Goals 2000 Community Partnerships (K-12, p 8)

Higher Education: Cooperative Education (84.055)

Howard University: Clinical Law Center

Howard University: Construction

Impact Aid: Facilities Maintenance (84.040)

* Impact Aid: Increases in Military Dependents (K-12, p7)

Indian Education: Special Programs (84.299)

Indian Education: Adult Education (84.062)

Indian Education National Activities

* Innovative Elementary School Transition Projects (k-12, p 10)

Innovative Projects for Community Service (84.116)

* International Education Comparative Analyses (K-12, p9)

Law School Clinical Experience

Legal Training for the Disadvantaged

Literacy Training for Homeless Adults

Middle School Teaching Demonstration Programs

* Minority-Focused Civics Education (K-12, p9)

National Board for Professional Teaching Standards

* National Mini Corps Program (Post Sec, p. 8)

National Occupational Information Coordinating Committee (No CFDA)

* National Student Savings Program (Post Sec, p. 9)

* National Teacher Academies (ProDev, p4)

Olympic Scholarships (84.301)

OPE: SFA Database and Information Line

* Patricia Roberts Harris Graduate Fellowship (Post Sec, p. 25)

* Presidential Access Scholarships (Post Sec, p. 9)

Programs for Indian Children/Demonstrations (84.299)

Programs for Indian Children/Professional Development (84.299)

* Removal of Architectural Barriers to the Handicapped (Constr, p. 3)

School, College, and University Partnerships (84.204)

School Facilities Infrastructure Improvement (84.284)

Small State Teaching Initiative

* Special Child Care Services for Disadvantaged College Students (Post Sec, p. 9)

* State and Local Programs for Teacher Excellence (ProDev, p3) "never funded"

State Postsecondary Review Program (84.267)

Teacher Corps

Teacher Research Dissemination

Territorial Assistance for the Virgin Islands

Territorial Teacher Training Assistance Program

* Title I Demonstrations of Innovative Practices (K-12, p7)

Training in Early Childhood Education and Violence Counseling

Training Programs for Educators: Alcohol Abuse (84.238)

Urban and Rural Education Assistance

Vocational and Adult Education: National Programs/Data Systems (SOICC)

* Workplace and Community Transition Training for Incarcerated Youth Offenders (K-12,p10)

* Women and Minorities Science and Engineering Outreach Demonstration (Post Sec, p 10)

* Women and Minority Participation in Graduate Education (Post Sec, p29)

U.S. Department of Education— Double-Counted or Items that are Not Programs:

Adult Education: National Programs (84.191) — not a separate program

Bilingual Education Field Initiated Research — not a separate program

Bilingual Education: Instructional Services (84.003)— double-counted

Capacity Building for Traditionally Underserved Populations (84.315)— not a separate program

Christa McAuliffe Fellowships — not a separate program

Elementary and Secondary Education Act: Evaluation and Studies — not a separate program

Even Start: Family Literacy in Women's Prisons Program — not a separate program

Even Start: Indian Tribes and Tribal Organizations (84.258) — not a separate program

Even Start: Migrant Education (84.255) — not a separate program

Even Start: Statewide Family Literacy Program — not a separate program

Federal Real Property Assistance Program (84.145) — not a separate program

FIPSE (Pennsylvania Telecommunications Network) — not a separate program

Foreign Languages Assistance (84.249)— double-counted

Fulbright-Hays Training Grants-Foreign Curriculum Consultants (84.020)— not a separate program

Fund for the Improvement of Education: Character Education Partnerships (84.215)— not a separate program

Fund for the Improvement of Education: Recognition Programs (Blue Ribbon Schools) (84.215)— not a separate program

Fund for the Improvement of Education: Student Assessment Initiative (84.215)— not a separate program

Gallaudet University: Endowment Grant (84.994K)— not a separate program

Howard University: Endowment Program — not a separate program

Howard University, Howard University Hospital — not a separate program

Howard University: Research — not a separate program

Impact Aid: Federal Acquisition of Real Property — double-counted

Indian and Native Hawaiian Vocational Education (84.259) — not a separate program

* Interlibrary Cooperation and Resource Sharing (p3)(84.035) deauthorized

International: Overseas - Doctoral Dissertation (84.022) — not a separate program

International: Overseas - Faculty Research Abroad (84.019) — not a separate program

International: Overseas - Group Projects Abroad (84.031) — not a separate program

National Assessment of Educational Progress (84.999)— double-counted

National Assessment Governing Board—advisory board, not a program

National Education Dissemination System — not a separate program

National Education Goals Panel—advisory board, not a program

National Institute on Disability and Rehabilitation Research (84.133)— not a separate program

NIDRR: Mary Switzer Fellowships (84.133)— not a separate program

NIDRR: Miscellaneous — not a separate program

NIDRR: Outreach to Minority Colleges and Universities (84.133)— not a separate program

NIDRR: Peer Review — not a separate program

NIDRR: Rehabilitation Service: American Indians with Disabilities (84.250)— not a separate program

NIDRR Research Training — not a separate program

NIDRR: Small Business Innovation Research — not a separate program

Regional Education Laboratories — double-counted

Rehabilitation Act Evaluation — not a separate program

Rehabilitation Services: Service Projects — double-counted

Smith Hughes Vocational Education Permanent Appropriation— not a program

IDEA: Program for Severely Disabled Children (84.086)— double-counted

Vocational Education: Indians Set-Aside (84.101)— not a separate program

Other Agencies—Unfunded and misidentified items

* 1890's Buildings and Facilities Program (Constr. p. 1)—unfunded

*Academic Research Infrastructure (ARI) (Constr, p2)—unfunded

* ADAMHA Small Instrumentation Program Grants (OMB 1&2, p 6)—deauthorized

Appalachian Vocational and Other Education Facilities and Operations (23.012) (ARC)— deauthorized in 1976

Arizona Historical Documents Education Foundation (GSA) This was a one-time ear-marked appropriation in GSA's 1995 appropriation bill for a construction project.

* Assistance for Delinquent and At-Risk Youth, (K-12, p11)—unfunded.

* Basic, Applied, and Advanced Research in Science and Engineering (Post Sec, p. 12)—deauthorized

* Basic and applied scientific research (Research, p. 5)—deauthorized

* Bilingual Vocational Instructor Training (K-12, p28)—unfunded

* Biometry and Risk Estimation: Health Risks from Environmental Exposures (K-12, p45) — unfunded

* Centers of Excellence Bilingual and Bicultural Minority Pre-Faculty Fellowship Grants (ProDev, p5) This was a 2-year demonstration grant that ended in 1996. It will not be funded again.

* Child Development Associate Scholarships (ProDev, p11)—unfunded

* Christopher Columbus Fellowship Program (Post Sec, p. 8)— Since 1993, the Foundation has not received a federal appropriation.

Cooperative Extension Service (10.500)—not a program, but an administrative unit of USDA

* Department of Defense Dependent Schools (K-12, p6)—deauthorized

* Families and Children with Disabilities Support Act of 1994 (SS, p2)—unfunded

Federal Employment for Disadvantaged Youth: Part-Time (CFDA 27.003) (OPM)—deauthorized

* Federal Transit Managerial Training Grants (ProDev, p 7)—unfunded
* Federal Transit Grants for University Research and Training (Post Sec, p 14)—deauthorized
* Financial Assistance Program: Science Education and Technical Information (Post Sec, p. 19)—unfunded
* Grants for Mining and Mineral Resources and Research Institutes (Post Sec, p. 13) —deauthorized
* Health Services in the Pacific Basin (Post Sec, p. 36) —unfunded

Higher Education Strengthening Grants (10.211) — unfunded

Homeless Veterans Reintegration Project Labor, Veterans' Employment and Training — unfunded.

* Human Nutrition Information Service (OMB 1&2, p2) — deauthorized
* Independent Education and Science Projects and Programs (K-12, p15) — unfunded
* International Educational Exchange: Samantha Smith Memorial Exchange Program,(k-12, p. 12)—unfunded
* Job Training for the Homeless, Demo (p. 4)—unfunded
* Language Grant Program (ProDev, p6)—deauthorized
* Mental Health Clinical and AIDS Service-Related Training Grants (PostSec, p.39)—unfunded
* Minority Honors Training and Industrial Assistance Program (Post Sec, p 18)—deauthorized
* Minority Math Science Leadership Development Recognition (Post Sec, p. 19)—deauthorized
* Minority Undergraduate Training for Energy Related Careers (Post Sec, p 18)—deauthorized
* Museum Science Education Program (OMB1&2, p 1)—unfunded

National Council on Disability (CFDA 92.001)— this was a one-time publication on IDEA— not a program.

National Fire Academy Educational Program (CFDA 83.010) National Fire Academy (FEMA)—
This is an organizational unit of the U.S. Fire Administration, not a program.

* National Security Education Program (Post Sec, p. 5)—deauthorized

National Service Trust (Corp. Nat'l Serv)—This is not a program. It is an account at the U.S. Treasury.

* National Workforce Literacy Assistance Collaborative (p.4)— this was a pilot program and is now unfunded.

National Endowment for Children's Education Television (11.551) (DOC)—unfunded

Part D: Juvenile Gangs and Drug Abuse and Drug Trafficking (16.544) (DOJ)—not a separate program

Population Protection Planning (CFDA 83.514) State and Local Programs and Support (FEMA)—deauthorized

* Post-Vietnam Era Veterans' Educational Assistance (Post Sec, page 16)—deauthorized

Pre-Freshmen Enrichment (81.047) (DOE)—unfunded

* Pre-Service Teacher Enhancement Programs (Post Sec, p. 8)—unfunded
* Program for Study of Eastern Europe and the Independent States of the former Soviet Union—unfunded

Public and Indian Housing Family Investment Centers Program (14.861) —unfunded

* Science and Engineering Research Semester (Post Sec, p. 18)—unfunded
* Self Determination Grants: Indian Tribal Governments (SS, p3)—deauthorized

Shelter Survey Technician Program: Job Qualification Training, State and Local Programs and Support Directorate (FEMA)—unfunded

Teacher Research Associate Program (TRAC) (DOE)—unfunded

Technical Assistance Program (No CFDA) (HHS)—unfunded

* Training and Public Awareness Projects in Technology Related Assistance for Individuals with Disabilities (Training, p. 15) —unfunded

* Training and Technical Assistance: Indian Tribal Governments (ProDev, p6)—unfunded

* Transition Assistance Program (p. 1)—unfunded

* Transitional Living for Runaway and Homeless Youth (SS, p 5)—deauthorized

Urban Youth Corps (No CFDA, No description) (DOT)—unfunded

* Used Energy-Related Laboratory Equipment Grants (Post Sec, p 17)—unfunded

* Vista: Literacy Corps (Gen Ed, p11)—unfunded

* Vocational Training for Certain Veterans Receiving VA pensions (p. 11) VA is not allowing anymore people into this program and intends to phase it out once the last person has completed the program.

* Workers Technology Skill Development Act (p. 3)—deauthorized

* Young Scholars (K-12, p 18)—This program is no longer funding new proposals

* Youth Conservation Corps (K-12, p. 9)—unfunded

* Youth Fair Chance (under Job Training Partnership Act) (p.4)—FY95 funding rescinded; no further appropriation; authorization expires at the end of FY97.

ENCLOSURE II

Table II.1: Education Department Programs With Direct Instruction Assistance for K-12 Students as the Primary Purpose With FY 97 Grant Amount (in Millions)

Count	CFDA[a] no.	Program name	Formula grants	Discretionary grants[b]	Other[c]	Targeted beneficiaries
1	84.003	Bilingual Education		X ($157)		Limited-English-proficient individuals
2	84.010	Title I Grants to Local Education Agencies (Title I Basic and Concentration)	X ($7,300)			At-risk children
3	84.011	Migrant Education--Basic State Grant Program	X ($300)			Children of migrant workers
4	84.013	Title I Program for Neglected and Delinquent Children	X ($39)			Children in state correctional institutions or state community day schools
5	84.027	Special Education--Grants to States	X ($3,109)			Children with disabilities aged 3-21
6	84.048	Vocational Education--Basic Grants to States	X ($1,016)			Secondary school, post-secondary, and adult students
7	84.162	Immigrant Education	X ($100)			Immigrant children in public and private schools
8	84.165	Magnet Schools Assistance		X ($95)		Students in magnet schools
9	84.203	Star Schools		X ($30)		Students and teachers
10	84.243	Tech-Prep Education	X ($100)	X		Secondary/postsecondary technical education students

Title I Studies

- An analysis of Title I state performance reports for assessment results will be conducted annually. Baseline data for 1995-96 are included in a report, supported by the Department of education and recently published through the Council of Chief State School Officers. The National Assessment will include subsequent data for the 1996-97 and 1997-98 school years.

- A National Assessment of Educational Progress (NAEP) trend analysis and state-by-state comparison of student performance in high-poverty schools will be available in Summer 1998.

- An examination of trend data in urban school districts that looks at selected districts with 3 years of achievement results will be included in the National Assessment of Title I.

- Longitudinal information through the Longitudinal Evaluation of School Change and Performance (LESCP), supplemental with data from the National Longitudinal Survey of Schools (NLSS), will also include trends in student achievement. One-year change in student achievement results, collected through the LESCP, will first be reported in Spring 1999. The NLSS will report baseline results in Spring 1999.

- The LESCP mandated under Title I is evaluating the impact of the key features of Title I legislation on schools, classrooms, and students. The evaluation examines a specially selected sample of 71 Title I elementary schools and tracks the impact of key features of the new legislation- such as standards-based curriculum and schoolwide programs- on both instructional practices and student achievement. The content areas of central importance are reading and mathematics. The first baseline report, which focuses on classroom practices, will be available in early Summer 1998. Annual reports will follow, with a final report due in 2001.

- The National Longitudinal Survey of Schools will complement the LESCP with a nationally representative survey examining how well Title I schools are implementing standards-based improvements. The study will also look at the extent to which schools use their outcome data to change classroom practice and how they measure progress continuously. The first and second interim reports are due in Spring and Fall 1998. A final report will be submitted in 2000.

- Baseline and Follow-up Studies of State-Level Planning and Implementation of Title I and other Federal Programs provide information regarding the planning process and early implementation of Title I, other state-administered programs under Improving America's Schools Act (IASA), and Goals 2000. Key issues include the process of developing state plans, setting standards, implementing accountability systems, and providing support to districts. The final report for the baseline study is expected in August 1998. The follow-up study will collect information in Fall 1998, and a final report is due in early 1999.

- An Evaluation of Federal Efforts to Assist School Reform has collected indicators, from the customers' perspective, of the federal government's performance in promoting improved state-, local-, and school-level practices under Title I and other federally supported efforts. How the filed has responded to the Department of Education's new authority to waive statutes and regulations is a particular focus. A final report, Reports on Reform from the Field, was released in Fall 1997.

- Study of Local Implementation will analyze districts' implementation of Title I and other federally supported efforts. The study will focus on issues related to local planning and implementation of federal programs-specifically standards and assessments, professional development, parental involvement and community engagement, and targeting. The study will be completed in Spring 1999, with data available in early Winter 1998.

- An Evaluation of Title I Participation of Private School Students surveyed a nationally representative sample of districts and private school representatives to examine the issues in allocation procedures and consultation regarding the participation of private school students. A final report was transmitted to Congress in July 1998.

- A Title I Targeting Study is examining how 17 of the largest districts allocate Title I funds to schools, the poverty data used to determine eligibility, and exceptions made to the rules governing allocations. An examination of changes in how districts allocate funds and the effects of individual targeting provisions will draw upon existing LEA records from as sample of districts. A final report is expected in Fall 1998.

- A targeting and Resource Allocation Study will examine how Title I and other federal resources are used at the school and district levels' how the allocation and use of resources varies by poverty; how resources are allocated for specific strategies emphasized in the law (e.g., schoolwide programs, professional development, and parent involvement); how resource allocation decisions are made; and the share of funds used for administration, instruction, and other functions. A contract for the study was awarded in fall 1997, and a final report is due in January 1999.

- The Study of Barriers to Parent Involvement presents findings on common barriers to effective parent involvement in Title I schools. It also reports on policies and programs that have overcome these barriers and improved parent involvement and practitioners and policymakers follows from the findings. The study was completed in winter 1997.

- The Study of the Impact of Title I Schoolwide Programs on Migrant Children examines the extent to which schoolwide programs affect learning opportunities for migrant students. Because schoolwide programs enable all students to benefit from Title I resources, these programs may facilitate access to services for migrant students. At issue, however, is the concern that the unique needs of migrant students may not be met. An interim report was submitted to the Congress in January 1998, with a final report to follow in Summer 1998.

State Administrative Costs for Formula Grant Programs
($ in millions)

Program	1997 Approp.	Max Percent for Admin.	Amount for Admin.
Goals 2000	$476	4.00%	$19.0
Title I LEA Grants	7,194	1.00%	71.9
Even Start	102	5.00% *	5.1
Title I Migrant	305	1.00%	3.1
Title I N&D	39	1.00%	0.4
Eisenhower Prof. Dev.	310	5.00% *	15.5
Title VI	310	3.75%	11.6
Safe & Drug-Free/SEAs	415	4.00%	16.6
Safe & Drug-Free/Governors	104	5.00%	5.2
Voc. Ed. (Basic Grants, Tech-Prep)	1,110	5.00%	55.5
Adult Education	340	5.00%	17.0
IDEA State Grants	3,108	5.00%	155.4
IDEA Preschool	360	5.00%	18.0
IDEA Infants & Families	316	no limit	?
TOTAL (not including IDEA Infants)	14,173	2.70%	382.7
TOTAL, ESEA programs	9,255	1.40%	129.6

* Authorization allows funds set aside at the State level to be used for technical assistance or other activities in addition to State administration.

NOTE: In all cases, the percentages shown are the maximum amounts that States can use for administration. Some States will use smaller amounts for some programs. On the other hand, the maximum amount for a few programs is actually slightly higher than what is shown because the statute allows States to reserve X% or $Y, whichever is greater; this will have only a minimal impact on the overall totals, but allows the smallest States to use, for administration, a portion significantly greater than the national averages.

PATSY T. MINK
Member of Congress

ROBERT C. SCOTT
Member of Congress

RON KIND
Member of Congress

HAROLD E. FORD, JR.
Member of Congress

ISBN 0-16-057542-7

9780160575426
EDUCATION AT A CROSSROADS WH/

Y0-EFN-142